Our Controversial Bible

by

Claus Westermann

Translated and Edited by

Darold H. Beekmann

AUGSBURG PUBLISHING HOUSE
Minneapolis, Minnesota

OUR CONTROVERSIAL BIBLE

This volume is a translation of UMSTRITTENE BIBEL, © *1960 Kreuz-Verlag, Stuttgart, Germany.*

Unless otherwise indicated, Scripture quotations are from the Revised Standard Version of the Bible (RSV), copyright 1946 and 1952 by the Division of Christian Education of the National Council of Churches.

"It would give me much joy if I were to discover that many a person with questions concerning the Bible had received through this book the courage to bring these questions into the open in order that the great dialogue of the Bible might come alive in our own discussions along the way."

CLAUS WESTERMANN

Translator's Preface

To label the Bible "controversial" might strike many as highly questionable. To the author of this book, such a label is anything but questionable; rather, it indicates that the Bible "is being taken seriously as a vital factor in the history and thought of our twentieth century." He writes out of a deep concern that "those persons with questions on their hearts concerning the Bible might receive the courage to bring these questions into the open in order that the great dialogue of the Bible might come alive. . . . "

As Prof. Westermann states in the epilogue to the German edition: "The purpose of this book is to assist those who seek a better understanding of the relationship between the Bible as the Word of God proclaimed in the preaching of the church and the Bible as it originated in the form of human words, in oral and written traditions, and thus open to scientific, historical interpretation."

"It is my hope that these lectures will enable more persons to become involved in what is only the beginning of a changing relationship between the scientific, critical interpretation of Scripture and the proclamation, teaching, and practice of the church. . . . "

This frankness concerning the human-historical nature of the Bible coupled with a deep pastoral concern for the life of the church and a profound reverence for the message of the living God which speaks through the pages of the Bible is reflected throughout the book.

To illustrate how modern biblical research (often known as "biblical criticism") has helped to uncover and illuminate the essential message of the Bible, the author applies some of its tools, such as "form criticism," "literary criticism," etc., to certain especially controversial subjects with which the Bible deals. To those accustomed to a chronological approach to the Bible, there may seem to be little relationship between these subjects as they appear here, but there is a direct relationship, and this should become apparent when we follow the author as he moves back and forth between the Testaments, here showing that a New Testament event can properly be understood only in the light of its Old Testament background, there pointing out how the true meaning of an Old Testament phenomenon is revealed as it reaches its fulfillment in a New Testament occurrence. In this way the author also illustrates the relationship between the Old and New Testaments and the overall unity of the Bible, without superimposing upon it an artificial structure or an overriding theme.

This book grew out of a series of lectures originally presented over the South German Radio. Because the German edition closely followed the manuscript used in the oral presentation, editing was necessary, as well as considerable freedom in translation into English. This is reflected not only in the translation of certain words and phrases but also in the deletion of some elaborations and explanatory comments which were proper for an oral presentation but appeared redundant on the printed page. Some comments have also been added to the text where further explanation seemed advisable. To have noted all these internal changes would have been impractical and distracting. However, great care was exercised so as not to intentionally violate the author's original meaning or intent.

The Translator's Notes have been added primarily for the benefit of the layman who is just beginning to make his way through the field of modern biblical studies. Where Scripture is quoted, the Revised Standard Version has been followed, unless otherwise indicated by a footnote. An attempt has been made to document all scriptural references and to footnote all references to works by other authors. The Index of Scripture Quotations and the Selected Bibliography are further additions to the German original. All these changes and additions have been made with the approval of the author; nevertheless, I assume full responsibility for any inaccuracies which they may contain.

I wish to acknowledge my indebtedness to my wife for her many helpful suggestions and her patient understanding during the time when this translation was being completed.

DAROLD H. BEEKMANN

Contents

Chapter 1

Our Controversial Bible

In any present-day gathering where a story from the Bible is read—whether it be the Christmas story, the account of the Israelites passing through the Sea of Reeds,[1] or the report of Christ's ascension—there generally are those who ask, be it quietly or emphatically, openly or secretly, "Did it really happen that way?" Though it is true that even in the twentieth century there are many who still simply accept the stories as they are recorded in the Bible, even these believing persons should be vitally interested in the question because it troubles many whom they would lead to faith. We cannot keep modern man from raising such questions any more than we can pretend that such questions are not being raised. Dare we consider this questioning a sign of promise?

Whether they deal with the feeding of the multitude, the conquest of Canaan, the raising of a dead man, or the authorship of the Psalms, the questions vary greatly in origin and scope. Still, they all point to the fact that the Bible is controversial. This is true of its authenticity and reliability, as well as of its significance for the people of our time and its value for our changing world.

This certainly is not a new development, but until recently such inquiry generally was interpreted as a step away from the Bible or out of the church. It appeared that the church had to preserve

---

[1] Translator's Note: This is the more accurate and now widely accepted translation of the Hebrew *yôm sûf* used in Exodus 13:18. Cf. *The Torah*, a New Translation of the Holy Scriptures According to the Masoretic Text (Philadelphia: The Jewish Publication Society, 1962).

1

a faith in the Bible which would not even allow such questions to be raised. Great pains were taken to protect it from all possible doubt and criticism. This was right and proper during a period of transition when, to a great extent, the church lived by the faith of its fathers.

Now this transitional period appears to be drawing to a close. We are beginning to see this controversial Bible as the living Bible; to say that it is controversial is to say that it is being taken seriously. Precisely because it is controversial it can make itself felt as a factor in the history and thought of our twentieth century.

"Biblical criticism," a catchword often used in this connection, is thus clarified. If it means to imply that man now has the power, through human reason or common sense, to criticize or pass final judgment on the validity of the Bible, then biblical criticism almost certainly should be rejected. However, if it means that as I read the Bible, my power of discernment (the heart of biblical criticism) is given active part, then reading the Bible critically is a necessity.

When Dietrich Bonhoeffer spoke of a world "come of age," as compared to the church and its teaching,[2] it was largely due to a new way of understanding the Bible. During the Middle Ages and well into modern times, the Bible not only was viewed as the record of the saving acts of God, but also as the history of mankind from Creation to Judgment Day. Lessing, who wrote "The Education of the Human Race" in 1780,[3] still was firmly convinced that *the* early history of all mankind was depicted in the Old Testament. That the Old Testament contains the earliest documents of human history seldom is asserted today. We now realize that the people of Israel were not the earliest people of the earth but a relatively late branch of the Semitic family. In fact, a thousand years of recorded history precedes the history of Israel.

---

[2] Translator's Note: Cf. esp. Dietrich Bonhoeffer, *Letters and Papers From Prison*, revised edition (New York: The Macmillan Co., 1967). Cf. also *Die Mündige Welt*, IV Vols. (containing essays on Bonhoeffer's theology (Munich: Chr. Kaiser Verlag, 1955-63). Some of these are now available in *World Come of Age*, Ronald G. Smith, ed. (Philadelphia: Fortress Press, 1967).

[3] G. E. Lessing, "The Education of the Human Race," in *Lessing's Theological Writings*, Henry Chadwick, ed. (London: Adam & Charles Black, 1956), pp. 82-98. Translator's Note: Lessing was a German philosopher whose study of the Gospels as historical documents helped open the way for the scientific-historical approach to the Bible so common today.

The cosmology of the Bible presents a similar case.[4] Until recent times, the cosmology of the Bible was automatically considered just as valid as what the Bible had to say about Jesus Christ. Today, however, it is stressed that the purpose of the Bible is neither to present the early history of mankind nor to depict the cosmology of the ancient world. We recognize that our improved knowledge in these areas in no way affects the validity of the Bible, but it does result in a new approach to learning from the Bible.

In our day we no longer can say that questioning for the sake of understanding, or seeking a connection between our concept of reality and the often foreign words and narratives of the Bible, is either questionable or harmful to our understanding of the Bible. Recognition of the Bible as the Word of God, directed to us and valid for us, demands such questioning. In fact, the essential sign of unbelief in our time is the silencing of all questions directed at the Bible.

The typical unbeliever of our day no longer is interested in whether or not this or that incident took place exactly as related in the Bible. The period of passionate disputes over biblical facts is ending, or already has ended. Critical questions now directed at the Bible are moving more toward faith rather than toward unbelief. In our world a Bible that is not controversial would be a Bible that had been silenced.

In contrast to other sacred books in the history of religion, the Bible simply reports a happening. The chain of events, beginning with Abraham and continuing through the kings and prophets to Jesus and Paul, is never sealed and safeguarded in a sacred realm but is always interwoven with the occurrences of secular history. Consequently, in the events the Bible reports, every word spoken as well as every deed performed is controversial. Not one word of God is protected from inquiry and objection.

The vitality of the Word of God proves itself in the fact that it

---

[4] Translator's Note: Cosmology refers to a branch of science which has to do with the orderly structure of the universe. The Bible (and the ancient world) took for granted that the universe (cosmos) was made up of three definite parts: heaven, earth, and underworld. (Ex. 20:4). They believed that the firmament extended above the earth like a huge dome, holding back the waters above and supporting the abode of the gods (Gen. 1:6-8). The earth itself stood upon pillars which were sunk into the waters below (Psalm 24:2 and 104:5). Sheol, the abode of the dead, was located underneath these underground waters.

does raise questions and doubts, that it is attacked and rejected, that it is opposed by the majority, even the pious majority—the Bible itself views this as an essential element of the Word become flesh: "He came to his own and his own received him not" (John 1:11).

Continuous acceptance of the Bible has kept this vitality concealed during the greater part of the history of the Christian West. If today the Bible again is open to question, this can only be welcomed by those who recognize it as the living Word. To them the Bible is God's precious and costly, sustaining and liberating Word precisely because as they read it they take up the questions of those who question, the doubts of those who doubt, and the searchings of those who search. They take the Bible's historical character just as seriously as its divine-revelatory character.

In the past it generally appeared that the preaching and teaching of the church dealt only with the divine character of the Bible, while all scientific-theological efforts were applied solely to its human character. This simple separation can no longer be justified. The church must come to terms with these critical questions directed at the Bible, even as biblical research cannot continue without regard to the question of whether or not the Bible is the Word of God.

However, if we question whether the biblical account of an event corresponds to what actually happened, whether it is historical or not, we are led to a further question: What gave rise to the account and how did it come to us? Here the simple conclusion that the Bible is right after all, is of as little help to us as the assertion that this or that biblical account is unhistorical. Here we are dealing with a very complex question, and anyone concerned about this question must be willing to listen for a while and then join in the pursuit which leads down the path of such inquiry.

Let us take the narrative of Peter's call to discipleship, recorded for us in Mark 1, Matthew 4, and Luke 5, varied in form but with several similar characteristics. This narrative received its form from a small circle of common people where it was transmitted orally for a long time before it was recorded sometime after the death and resurrection of Jesus. It was orally transmitted in Aramaic, the language Jesus spoke; it was recorded in Greek and is still available to us today in that form. But in the church it existed in Latin for centuries before it was translated into the languages of Europe.

Thus the narrative was continuously entering different historical and intellectual environments, each generation hearing it anew in its own intellectual world.

How was this possible? What force carried the narrative over all these changes and differences into our present time? It certainly was not the oral and written transmitting, the translating, recording, and printing. These were secondary and accessory. The story of the call of Peter and the other disciples has come to us because it is part of a Gospel, part of the glad tidings. This story would have been forgotten long ago had it not been for this Gospel, preached and read in the services of worship, taught and learned in the church throughout the ages.

However, we still have not dealt with the most important question: How did the event of the call of the disciples come to be a narrative at all? Again we must give the same answer: From the outset this narrative came into being as part of a message, and it was put into narrative form because a message must be passed on. We cannot understand the narrative of the call of the disciples until we see it as part of this whole, as part of the message, the Gospel.

Chapter II

What Is a Gospel?

We know, in general, that the word "Gospel" means good news, glad tidings, a joyous message. But what should this mean with regard to such a complex literary work as the Gospels? For them to constitute a message in the actual sense of the word would be impossible, for a message must be brief. What a joyous message actually consists of is clearly shown in the Christmas story. The statement of the angel is a message; the angel is the messenger. From this one can assume that the *core* of the Gospels is a message and that the Gospels should be understood as a great fugue on one brief, simple theme with that theme being the message.

That this is the case can be concluded from the use of the word "gospel" throughout the New Testament, as well as from the structure of the Gospels themselves. The Gospels are neither biographies nor textbooks; rather, they are extensions or elaborations of a message.

To say that the Gospels are not biographies indicates that a "Life of Jesus" cannot be constructed from them. Such attempts were made again and again during the last two centuries, but all failed because they missed the essence and purpose of the Gospels. Albert Schweitzer's *The Quest of the Historical Jesus* [1] is a dramatic illustration of such an attempt. It demonstrates that the very thing everyone sought—the exact form and image of Jesus of Nazareth as he lived and moved on earth—was unattainable. Thus the conviction became generally accepted that one cannot extract from the Gospels an exact portrayal of the life of Jesus. In books about

---

[1] Albert Schweitzer, *The Quest of the Historical Jesus,* trans. by W. Montgomery (New York: Macmillan Co., 1948). First German edition, 1906.

Jesus which have appeared since then—such as those by Rudolf Bultmann, Martin Dibelius, Günther Bornkamm, etc.[2]—any attempt at an all-conclusive presentation of the life of Jesus has been waived from the very beginning. And this, we dare say, has brought us closer to the actual essence of the Gospels.

The fact that the Gospels are not biographies means that they do not attempt to be records of history, in the sense that history is a detailed and accurate account of specific events, and should never be evaluated as such. Rather, the Gospels interpret events, outlining their significance, and therefore should never be evaluated as one would evaluate a historical record. That this is vital to understanding the Gospels is evident from the Old Testament where there are clearly distinguishable historical and prehistorical narratives. The first specifically historical narrative is encountered in Israel at the beginning of the United Monarchy in the eleventh century B.C. The court history of David (2 Sam. 9 to 1 Kings 2), for example, is definitely a historical account, while stories of the judges, or the story of the wandering in the wilderness are not historical presentations in the true sense of the word.

However, this distinction should by no means be understood as a value judgment. It is merely based on the fact that narrative accounts of events from various periods and communities can be quite different. The forms in which these events are presented in the Gospels are determined by the circles from which they originated. That a historical presentation should come from the circle of the disciples or from the other close followers of Jesus is not to be expected and would hardly be possible. Were we here to encounter an explicitly historical form of presentation, it would be highly questionable.

It would signify a misunderstanding of the Gospels if we were to evaluate the reports of these humble men with the same criteria which we would apply to the *Annals* of Tacitus [3] and inquire into

---

[2] Rudolf Bultmann, *Jesus and the Word* (New York: Scribner's, 1958). First German edition, 1939. Martin Dibelius, *Jesus* (Philadelphia: Westminster Press, 1949). First German edition, 1939. Günther Bornkamm, *Jesus of Nazareth* (New York: Harper & Row, 1956).

[3] Translator's Note: Tacitus was a Roman historian who wrote around the turn of the first century. His *Annals* are among the few extra-biblical writings from this early period that make any mention at all of Christ and the Christian movement.

the historicity of the events they report. For example, the Gospels report many events such as the Passion history or the call of the disciples three times, four times, and even oftener. This is not typical of history-writing; rather, it indicates the attesting to an occurrence by more than one witness.

Neither should the Gospels be viewed as textbooks. Their main purpose is not to teach a religion or set of moral standards, nor do they present the ideas or thoughts of Jesus and his disciples. Throughout the history of the Christian church the attempt has been made to extract from the Gospels their essential thought content and to formulate this in terms of abstract thoughts and ideas. One heard of Jesus' "kingdom of God idea," his "ethic," and the "God-concept" in the Gospels. All these attempts missed the real point of the Gospels—the conveyance of a message. In contrast to this, there is a growing emphasis today on the "kerygma" that is, the proclamation, the preached word, in presenting the Gospels' message.

If the core of the Gospels is message, then we must ask, "What is a message?" Let us take the classical example of a victory message such as, "The Greeks have conquered." Is that the real message, detached from the situation of those who awaited the messenger, detached from the tension and excitement, from the cry of the approaching messenger and the weeping or cheering of those who heard that cry? Is the mere content of the message the message itself? It most certainly is not, and in the same way we must say that the mere content of the Gospel is not the Gospel. The message of the coming of the Savior *cannot* be detached from the event of his coming. One could say it this way: A message never can be reduced to a mere statement.

The Gospels want to be messages from God, or messages of an event in which God has acted. It is part of their nature as messages that they came from God.

Why do we say that God sends messengers, and what does that mean? Such a statement presupposes a distance between God and man which the message is to span. But is it not part of God's nature that he is omnipresent? What kind of distance is this that can be spanned only through messages and messengers?

In the Old Testament we are told that the distance was not always there. It sounds very simple, one might say primitive, when at the beginning of the Bible God's nearness to man is so described that God goes about in the garden which he has made for man and there speaks with man. Yet this simple language expresses something of lasting importance, namely, that the distance between God and man is not right, not normal. It was not initiated by God; it was of man's doing. Man has alienated himself from God.

In the early narratives of the Bible God speaks to individual men so directly that actual conversations between God and men are reported, as were those between God and Abraham and God and Moses. This gradually ceased. The change had begun to take place by the time of Moses, and by the time of the prophets God no longer spoke arbitrarily to men but only to those whom he called to carry out a special mission to the rest of his people. Thus the Bible indicates that this alienation from God, which makes a message necessary and significant, is confined to the history of mankind.

It was for this reason that the message of Jesus Christ came "in the fullness of *time*." This message belongs at the end of the list of God's messages in the Old Testament. It, too, deals with this same alienation, but it differs from the earlier messages from God in that it is God's final, all-conclusive message until the end of the world. This character of finality is expressed in the Gospels by the fact that their message deals with an event in which God himself entered the realm of history. The message of Jesus Christ is not alone a summary of what Jesus proclaimed; rather, it is the message that in him and in what is reported about him the distance between God and man has been overcome for all time. This is what Jesus was referring to in the words with which he began his ministry, as recorded in Mark:

> *Jesus came into Galilee, preaching the gospel of God, and saying, "The time is fulfilled, and the kingdom of God is at hand, repent, and believe in the gospel"* (Mark 1:14-15).

The significance of a message really can be understood only by returning to the time when the only possibility for spanning distances was through human words. The messenger had to impress the message upon his memory and then report it, word for word, without any change, to those to whom it had been addressed. Then, perhaps after a journey of days or weeks, the messenger would stand before those to whom the message had been sent.

The actual giving of the message, usually in the presence of witnesses, would become a festive occasion. The words of the message would be received with intense excitement. They would long be remembered and, depending upon their significance, they would be handed down for a long time in the circle in which they had been received.

Not only the message of Israel's prophets but also the message of the New Testament, the words and deeds of Jesus as recorded in the Gospels, must be viewed against the background of this ancient means of communication. The disciples of Jesus, Jesus himself, and the writers of the Gospels were several centuries closer to this period in human history than are we.

Immediately preceding God's message in the Gospels, however, is the history of his message in the Old Testament.

Chapter III

God's Message in the Old Testament

It is an exciting history that we have to present here, a history that excludes no area of human experience. We can survey it best from the end, from the angel's Christmas message to the shepherds in the fields in the middle of the night. For them the day of fulfillment had dawned, the day awaited for centuries.

Over a thousand years earlier their fathers, driven by hunger, had wandered into Egypt. There they were forced into slavery until the day when one arose from their midst with a message from God promising them freedom and a new homeland. Because of this message they risked a long trek through the wilderness. They lost heart and murmured; they rebelled and were defeated, but the message remained constant. They entered the promised land and became a nation. However, this did not happen without severe setbacks, bringing them to the brink of annihilation. It was at this point that a messenger of God appeared to a young shepherd, a farmer's son, and called him to be the deliverer of his people (1 Sam. 16).

This message always had the character of the totally unexpected. Those who received it never seemed to possess any of the prerequisites normally associated with someone through whom great things are to be accomplished. Among these recipients of the message one encounters the fearful, the very young, the uneducated, schemers, imposters, an adulterer, and even a murderer. Yet, the message never appeared in complete isolation; it always attached

11

itself to past history in which God's word to his people had proved itself miraculous and powerful. Regardless of its unexpected nature, it was always heard within the context of a promise, a covenant, God's special relationship with his chosen people.

God's message took another direction in Israel's early history. We see a woman in deep sorrow because she cannot bear a child, and she knows no other honor or good fortune than that of being a mother. Again a messenger from God appears, bringing her the glad tidings that she shall bear a son (Gen. 18-21). The early books of the Old Testament are marked throughout by a chain of such messages concerning the birth of a child which turns a woman's sorrow into exuberant joy

It is clear that these two events—the one dealing with the announcement of salvation for the people and the other with the announcement that a child is to be born—were fulfilled in the first two chapters of the Gospel of Luke telling of the annunciation and birth of Jesus and John the Baptist. Only against this background can we begin to understand what these chapters really attempt to say.

The question of whether these events are historical or legendary misses the point entirely. In the Old Testament, the two lines of the message just referred to, that is, the birth of a child and the call of a deliverer through the direct appearance of a messenger, are limited to the early traditions of the people of Israel. Such messengers no longer appear during the actual historical period of Israel's existence, beginning with the introduction of kingship in the eleventh century B.C.

The circle of early Christians from which this story in the Gospel of Luke arose lived so completely in the Old Testament that it unknowingly brought to life again, with an amazing freshness and clarity, the speech, the way of thinking, and the forms of expression from this early period. Here we have an exceptionally beautiful example of genuine, living tradition. Thus the meaning of these two chapters becomes clear; an arc is cast from the event of Christ's coming to earth, back to the beginnings of the people of Israel, and we hear the announcement of the final fulfillment of that long period of waiting.

When we arrive at the actual historical period of Israel's existence, God's message to his people takes an astounding turn. The prophets begin proclaiming their message of judgment. Christ's message of salvation can be fully understood only against the background of this message of judgment which the prophets were commanded to proclaim to their people as the Word of God.

This message of judgment arrives when the people of God, for the first time in their history, have become great and powerful. The moment the prophet Nathan steps before King David and, in the name of God, makes a charge against the king (2 Sam. 12), Nathan becomes a messenger of judgment. Thus we have the beginning of that period of Israel's history which finally reaches its end in the annihilating intervention of God against his own people. At first the message of judgment was intended only for kings and then only where they acted in contradiction to the ancient laws of God.

We know little about this early period of prophecy. In First and Second Kings it is mentioned only in brief episodes where the prophet simply utters a word and disappears again. However, recent studies have brought to light indications of the great significance of this early prophecy, which probably was closely related to Israel's worship. It is now becoming clear that during this period the proclamation of judgment was a rare exception, and that the task of the prophets was more closely associated with the proclamation of salvation. For example, in all probability, Amos, one of the first writing prophets, was once given the assignment of proclaiming salvation in the name of God. The visions in Amos 7 through 9 show how he appeared before God as intercessor for his people but then was compelled by God to assume the difficult task of being messenger of God's judgment.

With Amos begins the period in which the message of judgment is proclaimed not just to one individual, such as the king, but to the entire people of God. This period lasted one and one-half centuries. Imagine, for a moment, a church which for one and one-half centuries hears nothing but the proclamation of doom upon the nation to which it belongs. In the entire recorded history of mankind this is the only instance where we find such a period of one-sided emphasis on impending doom, even as there seems to be no parallel to the Gospel's message of salvation in Christ. The reason this message of judgment covered such a long period of time is found in the increasing and willful separation of the people from God. At the same time the reason also is found in the faithfulness of God to his people as they separated themselves from him in the most crucial areas of their life: in their politics, their social structure, and their worship.

This separation was not peculiar to Israel. It has been typical of all mankind in many different periods and circumstances. We know of no people or community on earth that did not at its beginning possess a religion. Whether it be the Near East, Central Africa, or North America, at one time or another all areas of life were rooted in a god-relationship and embraced by a religion. In each instance there followed a contrasting period in which the political, social, legal, and cultural were loosed from their religious moorings and made independent.

An example of this in Israel was the type of war she engaged in during her early history, a war understood to be divinely sanctioned, a war in which God took a direct part, a "holy" war which today is hardly imaginable. But by the time of David, war had become a secular action, separated from the realm of the sacred. Likewise, there emerged a secular law and an entire series of social institutions, such as the government, all entirely freed from the cult.[1]

The prophets recognized this secularization of politics, war, law, and society as a necessary development. Their charges were first raised when the people openly acted contrary to God's will, or when God's will was no longer taken into consideration. The prophets offered the people no new concepts of God, but with real passion they urged them to hold firm to what God already had revealed to them.

The entire judgment message of the Israelite prophets can be summarized under two main themes: (1) the announcement of judgment which runs with unnerving monotony through all the prophetic books from Amos to Jeremiah and Ezekiel, and (2) the charges upon which these announcements of judgment are based. Most of the charges were political, social, or legal.

However, the judgment message of the Israelite prophets also contained something which was to be of vital importance for the

---

[1] Translator's Note: Cult in this sense means the entire system of worship, including the various rites and ceremonies prescribed for such diverse occasions as anointing a king, sanctioning a war, dedicating a place of worship, offering a sacrifice, or observing a regular festival such as the Passover.

history of mankind. Here at *one* point we have a breakthrough in the development which in every other instance in human history has led to the estrangement of religion from all other areas of life. The messengers declare the sovereign rule of God also in those areas where man is disassociating himself from God.

In this judgment message the way is prepared for the salvation message of Jesus Christ. Only in this context does it become clear that Christ's message of salvation deals not only with what we call religion but with God's sovereignty over the whole of human existence. What the prophets had announced came to pass. The state fell, and the Promised Land became the property of one world power after another. It was during this catastrophe that the message changed from judgment to the proclamation of a new redemption. Out of the remnant of those who had been led into exile there now arose a new voice with a message from God, a voice anticipating God's joyous and liberating future. This unknown prophet of the Exile, whom we know as Deutero-Isaiah because his writings became attached to the Book of the Prophet Isaiah,[2] announces that God will come again to redeem his lost people.

The message of salvation had never been completely silenced in Israel, not even during the period of the judgment prophets. Isaiah, himself a messenger of judgment, announced with certainty the deliverance of Jerusalem. This he did twice while working in an apparently hopeless state of anxiety among an entire people and contrary to the disbelief of his king. Beside these prophets of judgment there always stood the prophets of salvation, and events seemed to support their prophecy rather than that of the prophets of judgment. As Israel journeyed down the path to destruction, there were signs that destruction was not the ultimate will of God. Nevertheless, the complete message of salvation did not appear until the arrival of Deutero-Isaiah, the messenger who was sent after the collapse of the monarchy.

No visible fulfillment followed Deutero-Isaiah's glowing, jubilant message of salvation. The exiles were allowed to return, Jerusalem was rebuilt, and the temple was restored, but this was a

---

[2] Translator's Note: That Isaiah 40-55 was written by this unknown prophet of the Exile is seldom questioned today. Whether chapters 55-66 also came from his pen or were perhaps the work of another unknown author, "Trito-Isaiah," still is open to question.

fragmentary fulfillment. The awaited time of salvation did not arrive. The new life of God's people was poor and constrained. They remained a people who walked in darkness.

And with that we once again find ourselves with the shepherds of the Christmas story, waiting in the fields. Into this waiting came the joyous message of Christ.

Chapter IV

The Gospels: Their Origin and Meaning

The Gospels, as we know them today, were written about a generation after the death of Jesus. The Gospel of Mark was written about 70 A.D., Luke and Matthew between 75 and 95 A.D., and the Gospel of John around 100 A.D. (according to Günther Bornkamm).[1] At first this time interval seems almost more than we can comprehend, for it was during the decades between the death and resurrection of Jesus and the writing of the Gospels that we discover the decisive advance of the message of Christ, as it spread from Jerusalem and the villages on the Sea of Galilee to Syria, Asia Minor, Greece, and Rome. Paul's entire ministry, for example, took place *before* the formation of the Gospels.

To understand the Gospels and their implications for our time, it is important to recognize that they originated as part of the movement that carried the Gospel, the good news, into the world. Added to the problem presented by the astonishing interval between the ascension of Christ and the writing of the Gospels was the problem of language. Aramaic was Jesus' native tongue, the language he used in his talks with the disciples and in his controversies with the Pharisees. The earliest narratives circulated concerning him also were in Aramaic. However, as the message made its way into the world, the transition into Greek was so complete that there remains for us today not even the slightest trace of the Aramaic antecedents to the Gospels, not even a manuscript from a later

---

[1] *Op. cit.*, Appendix I, "Introduction to the History and Sources of the Synoptic Gospels," pp. 213-220.

period. Had the tradition of Jesus of Nazareth remained within the Aramaic-speaking world, the Gospel would never have been handed down to us, Christianity would not have become a world religion, and Jesus of Nazareth would soon have been forgotten.

It is in this transition into the Greek, however, that we recognize the impetus behind the movement of the Gospel into the world, namely, the impulse of mission. The actual working of this force can no longer be accounted for historically. We can only accept "the mission and expansion of Christianity in the first three centuries" [2] as one of the greatest movements in human history, with an abundance of historical consequences. The formation of the Gospels was one of these consequences. The Book of Acts refers to something very basic to this movement when it says:

> *"For we cannot but speak*
> *of what we have seen and heard"* (4:20)

" . . . what we have seen and heard." This statement refers above all to the suffering, death, and resurrection of Jesus Christ for the salvation of the world. Later, the first open proclamation of these events introduced this movement in whose wake the Gospels were formed.

The significance of Jesus' resurrection for the Gospels can be understood in the light of an Old Testament phenomenon. The story of the two disciples on the road to Emmaus (Luke 24) shows a striking similarity to a whole group of Old Testament stories about people visited by a messenger from God. These stories all have one thing in common: The messenger is not recognized at his coming, only at his departure. In like manner, the Emmaus story describes the resurrection as part of everything associated with Jesus' coming. In Jesus of Nazareth there came to man an ambassador from God, one who walked entirely as a man among men: " . . . being born in the likeness of men. And being found in human form" (Phil. 2:7-8). He did not disclose his real identity, however, until his departure. Only then, through his death and resurrection, were the eyes of his disciples opened. Just as Jesus' Emmaus encounter with his disciples first became clear at his departure, so also his coming into

---

[2] Adolf von Harnack, *The Mission and Expansion of Christianity in the First Three Centuries,* now available in the Harper Torchbook Series (New York: Harper & Row).

the world first becomes clear when viewed from the end, from his resurrection.

For this reason, the death and resurrection of Jesus became the core of the message of salvation, and out of the missionary endeavors of the young Christian community, the Gospels gradually took form around this core.

Only one series of events from the life of Jesus is reported in its original context by all four Gospels: the events of Jesus' passion concluding with the resurrection. The very structure of the Gospels makes it clear that, from the beginning, Jesus' activity was directed toward this goal. While the Gospel of John is otherwise quite different from the first three Gospels, all four say essentially the same thing when speaking of these events and agree most clearly and directly with the preaching of the apostles, as recorded in the early chapters of the Book of Acts, and with the proclamation of Paul in his Epistles.

The message which Jesus himself proclaimed—the message of the arrival of the rule of God—is intricately related to this core element of the Gospels' message. Here the person of Jesus is not to be separated from his words. The coming of the rule of God takes place where he is and in what he says and does.

Collections of Jesus' sayings and accounts of his deeds gradually attached themselves to the story of his passion and took the form of a continuous account, presenting his ministry as an unbroken movement from his first appearance to his entry into Jerusalem. Originally there was no continuous account. Only as these sayings and events were joined together with the passion history to form a Gospel did they become arranged in this manner. To this day, no exact parallel to the Gospels has been found in all of world literature. One could say that the uniqueness of the Gospels is an indication of the uniqueness of the event they proclaim.

To my knowledge, the Book of Jeremiah is the only parallel to this literary form, and that is a limited and distant parallel. Like the Gospels, the Book of Jeremiah was constructed out of three basic elements: the words of the prophet, the account of his suffering, and the experiences relating to the proclamation of his words. Similar, also, is the fact that only a few unrelated incidents from Jeremiah's life are reported up to the point where he is taken captive during the siege of Jerusalem. It is at this point that the story of his suffering, of his "passion history," begins, and only these latter occurrences are reported as a continuous narrative. A further similarity is seen in the fact that individual collections of Jeremiah's sayings existed independently at first and only later were joined together in the account of Baruk, who could be described as a disciple.

Out of the early Christian community there arose a whole group of writings having this general literary form. In addition to the four in the New Testament, there were many others, as Luke plainly indicates in the foreword to his Gospel (Luke 1:1-4). From later times we know of a series of apocryphal Gospels,[3] including the recently discovered Gospel of Thomas,[4] which contains a few statements that possibly go directly back to Jesus. Today it is generally agreed that Mark is the oldest of the Gospels and that Matthew and Luke had access to Mark, in addition to a *Sourcebook of Sayings,* so called because it contained sayings of Jesus primarily. This *Sourcebook*[5] no longer exists as such but can be reconstructed for the most part from the material common to Matthew and Luke but lacking in Mark. In addition, Matthew and Luke contain large blocks of material unique to each, thus illustrating the continuing vitality of the Gospels' tradition, even to the time when these Gospels were written. These three Gospels are known as the Synoptics. They can be viewed together since they contain, in general, the same structure and content.

Nevertheless, each of the Synoptics remains an independent work with its own unique characteristics. The latest research has shown how the development of each Gospel reflects a particular situation with a particular interest. The Gospel of Mark has been called the "book of secret epiphanies" (Dibelius[6]) because it is character-

---

[3] Translator's Note: Apocrypha, from the Greek word meaning concealed, refers to secret writings produced by esoteric groups. It is used to designate those writings, especially from the period surrounding the New Testament, that are considered to be of dubious authenticity. For an English translation of the most important New Testament apocrypha cf. M. R. James, *The Apocryphal New Testament* (Oxford: Clarendon Press, 1928, reprinted 1950).

[4] Translator's Note: *The Gospel According to Thomas,* Coptic text established and translated by Guillamont, Puech, *et al.* (New York: Harper & Row, 1959). This is an early apocryphal Gospel discovered in Egypt in 1945. Among other things, it contains numerous legendary stories about Jesus' infancy.

[5] Translator's Note: This unknown sourcebook usually is designated as "Q," from the German word *Quelle* meaning "source."

[6] Martin Dibelius, *From Tradition to Gospel,* trans. by Bertram Woolf (New York: Scribner, 1935), p. 230.

ized by the tension between the breakthrough of God's victory in the coming of Christ and concealment of that victory in Christ's humility and suffering. In the Gospel of Matthew, the teachings and regulations of the church are already much more apparent. Here one can detect Christianity's conflict with Judaism by the many quotations from Old Testament prophecy which are interpreted as having reference to Christ. Luke's account differs from both Matthew and Mark in that the early Christians' expectation of an immediate end of the world recedes into the background and an emphasis on history becomes more predominant. Luke has been called the "first Christian historian" (Martin Dibelius).[7]

The structures of the first three Gospels give another indication of the differences between them. Mark most clearly illustrates how the whole was formed out of individual sayings and originally independent narratives. Connecting words and sentences are few and reserved. Matthew, with his interest in teaching, tends to take individual sayings and mold them into major discourses as, for example, in the Sermon on the Mount (Chapters 5 through 7) and the famous parable discourse (Chapter 13). An interest in history becomes apparent with Luke in his emphasis on chronological order and arrangement, even to the point of placing biblical events into the context of world history.

The Gospel of John is entirely different. Only the last part, the account of the suffering, death, and resurrection of Jesus, corresponds to the other three Gospels. In contrast to the short sayings and narratives of the Synoptics, John presents the ministry of Jesus in long discourses, introduced and illustrated by a few of Jesus' acts. This is no longer the simple reporting of an event by a witness. It is the transmission of a message penetrated by theological reflection and coined in the language of a particular circle. A reflection of this language in one of the recently discovered documents from the Dead Sea[8] reinforces the assumption that the circle around John the Evangelist had some connection with the circle around John the Baptist.

---

[7] *Ibid.*, pp. 11, 203, 210, 262 ff.
[8] Translator's Note: Here the author is referring to the *Rule of the Community* (the so-called *Manual of Discipline*). For further discussion and bibliography on the subject see: Raymond E. Brown, S.S., "The Qumran Scrolls and the Johannine Gospels and Epistles," in *The Scrolls and the New Testament*, Krister Stendahl, ed. (New York: Harper & Row, 1957), pp. 183-207.

The unique language of each of the four Gospels is apparent even in such details as the words from the cross recorded in each. One cannot avoid being amazed at the freedom in the early church which allowed the placing of several very different Gospels side by side. This clearly expresses the fact that those who speak through the Gospels are not historians; they are witnesses. In the gathering of evidence before a court, a variety of witnesses is not only expected but desired. The statements of the witnesses become credible precisely because each, in his own way, relates what he has seen and heard. That is the reason we have more than one Gospel in the New Testament.

Chapter V

The Formation of the Gospels

Thus far we have spoken only of the formation of the Gospels as a whole. To see something of how each Gospel came into being, we must start by picturing the beginnings of the Gospels as simply as possible. The story of the disciples on the road to Emmaus is introduced with these words, " . . . and talking with each other about all these things that had happened" (Luke 24:14). Thus began the tradition of Jesus of Nazareth; the eyewitnesses spoke of what they had seen and experienced. And indeed, such activity was not confined just to the disciples: "This report concerning him spread through the whole of Judea, and all the surrounding country" (Luke 7:17, cf. also Matt. 4:24, 9:26, 31). They spoke of him, friends and enemies alike, those who came to him and those who left him, those who were thankful and those who were only annoyed.

The Gospels in unison, even the much later Gospel of John, reflect the fact that during Jesus' entire ministry there was a constant shifting from enthusiastic agreement and support to passionate rejection or complete apathy. From the beginning he is depicted as a controversial figure. It is for this reason that the entire tradition concerning Jesus of Nazareth reverberates with a highly critical element. He is presented as one who experienced rejection and hostility much more than acceptance and recognition.

These early traditions took form, so to speak, under the open skies. Even as Jesus himself, as far as we can discern, spoke mostly in the out-of-doors, so the reporting of his deeds and the spreading

23

of his sayings also took place in the open, out on the streets and pathways, during a work break, on the way out to fish, or in the evening in front of the homes. The circle of those who told and retold these stories consisted of farmers and fishermen, craftsmen, publicans, housewives. All these sayings and stories have assumed the simple language of everyday life, and this language has been preserved in its final form in the Gospels. For instance, there is the parable which begins:

A *sower went out to sow his seed* (Luke 8:5).

Or the passage beginning,

And he saw two boats by the lake;
but the fishermen had gone out of them and were washing
their nets (Luke 5:2).

This language continued to play an important role as the Gospels made their way throughout the world. Today we are so accustomed to hearing these words and stories within the context of public worship that, without realizing it, we are influenced by this atmosphere whenever we hear or read, for instance, the story of the sower. Somehow the words strike us as being solemn and festive. Once we become aware of this influence of worship, the non-theological character of these stories and sayings becomes clear, and the simple, colloquial language begins to reflect a mysterious beauty and dignity that cannot be avoided. From the very beginning this has made it possible for these words to reach men of every status and position.

When Jesus of Nazareth moved from place to place throughout the countryside and spoke to people as he met them, his words were immediately received as a message. We see this in the fact that the tradition, as it has been handed down to us, is made up entirely of brief statements and sayings. The same is true of the accounts of Jesus' healing and other acts. The accounts are brief and contain only the most necessary details. They attempt nothing more than to give testimony to the authoritative power which had confronted those who were now bearing witness to these events.

Jesus also spoke in longer discourses. It is certain that the controversies he had with his opponents were not all as brief as recorded in the Gospels. But the extremely brief style of Jesus' sayings and accounts of his actions, as formulated in the Gospels, helps us to realize that his hearers listened to him as they would to a messenger who had come from a great distance. They looked to him as one who had power that came from somewhere else. Therefore, what they saw and heard they passed on in a most concise and clear fashion so that the sayings and reports could be remembered easily and passed on again, each as a living and independent unit in itself.

If we but listen, we will be mindful of the fact that these acts and sayings of Jesus once stood amid many others which no longer are known to us. With this in mind, we will take much more care in our interpretations and recognize that each of these sayings once had its own hour, its own situation which we no longer can discern, or, at best, discern only in vague outline.

Once we see each independent saying, each separate account, in its own right, we notice a conspicuously similar form which many of these sayings and narratives seem to possess. Most of them can easily be arranged into quite specific categories: parables, controversies, healing narratives, beatitudes, etc. Each category has its own distinct form. The context of these sayings and narratives as we find them in the Gospels today is not the result of their original chronological sequence and development, nor did it result from the rational unfolding of a teaching or theology. It is rather the consequence of a later development.

Instead, from many different directions and in many different ways, these sayings and narratives all focus on one central point. They often have no discernible relationship to each other; a parable can follow the healing of a blind man, then a controversy may appear. Their relationship to one another can be detected only from the common form which classifies them with others of a certain category. For example, in the parable of the kingdom the words "the kingdom of God is like . . . " used to introduce many of these parables clearly indicate that central point toward which most of them are focused. This hidden relationship can be graphically portrayed by drawing lines radiating in all directions from one central point. Only because of their relationship to this central point, to Christ speaking and acting as a man among men, do these narratives and sayings belong together.

With this we have uncovered the essential elements of the Gospels. These characteristic forms—the parables, healing narratives, sayings of Jesus concerning himself, controversy stories, sayings of Jesus' followers, laments, acclamations, miracle stories—are the original bearers of the traditions which reached their final formulation in the Gospels but which before that enjoyed a long and independent existence in oral form. These fixed forms, however, should not be viewed as literary creations, that is, the inventions of an author. They originated and existed only in communities where they had a definite and practical significance.

With this I have tried to illustrate what is known in the scientific, technical study of the New Testament as the "form critical" approach.[1] This approach to the New Testament is based especially on the works of Rudolf Bultmann and Martin Dibelius.[2] The significance of these two works rests in the fact that they have provided us with concrete literary evidence that the Gospels, written long after Jesus' death, go back to oral traditions and that these oral traditions must be much older than the Gospels and could not possibly have been the result of literary invention.

Evidence that the Gospels are not historical accounts of the life of Jesus has led to the discovery of their *essential* historicity. The characteristic forms in the Gospels point to the history of a community, and the relationship of all these forms to Jesus of Nazareth points to a decisive encounter between that community and Jesus.

Thus the early Christian witness to Jesus as the Christ and the proclamation of his message is once again brought closer to the simple narrative of the Gospels. In other words, the oral traditions

---

[1] Translator's Note: "Form criticism" is not a good translation of *Formgeschichte* (from history), for "criticism" suggests a negative, critical approach to Scripture. The primary concern of *Formgeschichte*, however, is not to be destructive or critical. It merely attempts to trace the history of biblical traditions and thereby to understand the literature of the Bible and the historical situation which gave rise to that literature. Thus the contribution of form criticism has been a positive one, leading to a clearer and more accurate understanding of the Bible's message, as demonstrated by Prof. Westermann in this volume. However, since the term "form criticism" has become so widely used in biblical studies, it would be merely pedantic to replace it here with the more correct "form history."

[2] Rudolf Bultmann, *History of the Synoptic Tradition* (New York: Harper & Row, 1963). First German edition, 1921. Martin Dibelius, *From Tradition to Gospel* (New York: Scribner, 1935). First German edition, 1919.

out of which the Gospels were formed all stand in close relationship to the life of the early Christian community, to her teaching, to her worship, and to her witness.

Now the question of the authenticity of the sayings of Jesus, as handed down to us in the Gospels, is cast in a new perspective. When we ask, "Were all the sayings of Jesus recorded in the Gospels really spoken by him in the exact form in which we find them today?" we are not taking into consideration the fact that the sayings of Jesus known to us are but a minute portion of all Jesus said and did during his lifetime, and the selection of Jesus' sayings which we possess stems not from Jesus himself but from his disciples.

Thus it becomes clear that there is no possibility of making a clear distinction between those sayings which Jesus spoke literally, as we read them today, and those sayings which were given their present form by the disciples in the early Christian community. The distinction between so-called authentic and inauthentic sayings of Jesus no longer assumes such importance. Those early Christian communities were just as directly the result of Jesus' activity as were his acts and his sayings. It is not possible to draw a sharp dividing line between the two.

The historicity of Jesus is not that of an isolated historical figure; it is rather the reality of One who provides us with a historical witness to himself. We should never exclude the possibility that this Christ could more directly confront us through a saying which first received its form in the early Christian community than through a saying taken directly from his lips, but which we no longer can understand because we do not know the situation out of which it arose.

Chapter VI

Israel's Early Traditions

In the Christmas story the angel's message, " . . . to you is born this day . . . a Savior" (Luke 2:11), is followed by a great multitude of the heavenly host praising God. One could not express more beautifully the fact that the response of praise to God belongs to the joyous message of salvation. The history of God's people in the Old Testament also began with a joyous message of deliverance; and there, too, the response was a hymn of praise.

We have spoken of the formation of the Gospels and have seen again and again their relationship to the Old Testament. However, it still is not clear how similar in origin the early traditions of the church of Jesus Christ and the early traditions of the people of Israel really are. The reason for the many parallels rests in the fact that both of these traditions were based upon a saving act of God which in turn became the starting point for the history of a community. There naturally remain some basic differences: one instance concerns an entire people and the other a religious community or congregation, with about a thousand years separating them.

As in the case of Gospel research, research into Israel's early traditions has resulted in the revolutionary discovery that these stories originated first as individual narratives and that these narratives were handed down orally for a long time before they finally were recorded and joined together into larger compositions. This approach was worked out above all by Herman Gunkel in his commentary on Genesis.[1] His work gave new direction to research

[1] Herman Gunkel, *Genesis* (Gottingen: Vanderhoeck & Ruprecht, 1922). The particularly significant preface to this monumental work has been published in English under the title *The Legends of Genesis*. Schocken Books, 1964.

which for a long time had placed its entire emphasis on the study of literary sources. The exposure of the literary sources behind the Pentateuch [2]—that great literary complex consisting of the first five books of the Bible—had also been a major accomplishment, the result of the efforts of many scholars over several generations. This movement reached its peak at the end of the nineteenth century in the work of Julius Wellhausen.[3]

Then came the recognition that the narratives concerning Israel's early history did not originate as literature, the work of writers and authors. Instead, these narratives grew out of the life of the people in all its variety, and were oral, not written, traditions. Determining this "situation in life" [4] is vital for an understanding of the traditions. As pilgrims journeyed to a shrine they were told the story of the origin of that shrine. When the tribal elders gathered, the great acts of God came alive in song and story. Fathers told their children how they had been brought to the land which now provided them with food and habitation. As gifts were brought before the altar, the recital of God's wonders and his gracious preservation became part of the sacrificial ceremony. To the proclamation of the commandments belonged the remembrance of the fulfillment of former prophecies.

These examples illustrate the fact that this new approach had a changing effect on the study of Israel's early traditions. The historical backgrounds of these traditions came to life and played a

---

[2] Translator's Note: from the Greek meaning "five volume (work)."

[3] Julius Wellhausen, *Prolegomena to the History of Israel* (New York: Meridian Books, 1957). First German edition, 1878. Translator's Note: It was largely the accomplishments of Wellhausen and his school which led to the unraveling of the four literary sources the author refers to later in this chapter. Although this approach, known as "source criticism," has led to abuses and has undergone modification and revision since the time of Wellhausen, it still is generally accepted that the four basic literary sources Wellhausen uncovered provided the basic content and structure of the Pentateuch.

[4] Translator's Note: This is becoming an increasingly common term used to designate, literally, the particular situations in the life of the people which gave rise to a certain tradition, for example, a victory celebration, a funeral, a marriage, or a pilgrimage. Naturally, this "situation in life" is an important key to understanding the original meaning and purpose of a particular unit of tradition. It also played a major part in determining the form of the tradition.

vital role in the narratives. It no longer was so important to fit a story, such as the formation of the covenant at Sinai, into a literary source. It became more important to understand this story in its original setting and to find that setting in which it once existed as living word, perhaps in a festival that renewed the covenant between God and his people.

This new direction of research coincided with the amazing and unexpected disclosures concerning Israel's pre-history and the world surrounding Israel. Discoveries were made that brought to light entire bodies of literature from Egypt, Mesopotamia, Syria, and Asia Minor. Excavations in the land of the Bible and its surrounding territory supported the biblical narratives with archeological evidence.

At this point we must understand the connection between the formation of the Old and New Testaments. Each began with the oral traditions that spanned the time between an event and the formation of a written record of that event. In the case of the Gospels, this time interval covered several decades; in the Old Testament it often was a matter of centuries. In each case it was the power of witness which made it possible to bridge such an interval. This process can be presented more simply and concretely in the Old Testament.

In both Testaments the saving act of God stands at the beginning. In the Old Testament this was the deliverance of a small band of Israelites out of Egypt. This act formed the basis for their becoming a people. Praise of God in response to this act became the nucleus of a historical confession of faith, a summary of the basic saving acts of God which was recited in public worship. This confession, in turn, formed the basis for the entire tradition of Israel's early history. All major episodes and themes of this early history are already present, already form a complete unity, in this confession or credo. This has been shown by Gerhard von Rad and Martin Noth in studies which have become standard works in the area of Pentateuchal research.[5] The entire monumental literary work which

---

[5] Gerhard von Rad, "The Problem of the Hexateuch" in *The Problem of the Hexateuch and Other Essays* (New York: McGraw-Hill, 1966), pp. 1-78. First German edition, 1938. Martin Noth, *Überlieferungsgeschichte des Pentateuch* (Stuttgart: Kohlhammer, 1948).

we know as the Pentateuch, or Torah,[6] resulted, then, from the praise of God's great acts and took form through a centuries-long process of expansion and growth around this nucleus.

As in the formation of the Gospels, the most important factor in the formation of the Pentateuch is the relationship of the individual oral traditions to the whole. It was the impetus of living testimonies to the redeeming acts of God which molded this profusion of diverse, independent traditions into a unified whole.

Naturally this can be only an approximate parallel along one particular line, fully aware of the essential differences between the Gospels and Israel's early traditions. One such difference is evidenced in the fact that although Israel's early traditions, as recorded in the Pentateuch, were gathered and handed down in several parallel accounts, in a later stage of development these accounts were woven together to form one continuous narrative. (In the strictest sense, this is true of only three of the accounts; Deuteronomy has remained a separate and independent book.)

There is a broader parallel in the fact that in both the Pentateuch and the Gospels it is common for the individual accounts to report the great acts of God by means of various witnesses placed side by side. In the joining together of these various sources or accounts, great care was taken to preserve this variety of testimony *(Mehrstimmigkeit des Zeugens)*. The majority of the individual narratives in the first four books of the Pentateuch are preserved in several forms—two, three, and even four. Often two or even three narratives are interwoven to form one, but the various seams usually can still be recognized, even though each original narrative is not preserved in its entirety. Two accounts of the same event sometimes have been

---

[6] Translator's Note: *Torah* is the Hebrew title for the first five books of the Old Testament as a unit. The English translation of this word is usually "law." Its actual meaning in the Old Testament, however, is much broader than "law" in the sense of legal enactments. It can refer to "divine instruction," "guidance," "direction," and even "revelation" (cf. Isaiah 8:16, 30:9, and 42:4). *Torah* points the way for the faithful Israelite and for the community of Israel in covenant with God. Therefore, not only the "laws" of the Pentateuch provide such guidance and direction, etc.; the entire history of God's dealings with Israel and with mankind serve to point the way. Thus *Torah* becomes the title that distinguishes these books containing the history of God's dealing with his people from the *Prophets* and the other *Writings* in the Old Testament (cf. Luke 16:16, Matt. 11:13, etc.).

placed several chapters apart. The call of Moses, for example, is related in Exodus 3 and again in Exodus 6.

In the exegesis [7] of these narratives, one must use a procedure similar to that used with the Synoptic Gospels—the various forms in which such a narrative appears must be compared. For example, the narrative of the banishment of Hagar cannot be properly understood unless the parallel accounts in Genesis 16 and 18 are compared. This similarity with the Synoptics is not merely external or accidental; in both instances, the variety (Mehrstimmigkeit) of the witness to what God has done is an essential part of the whole tradition.

It is striking how this parallel is continued in the case of Deuteronomy and the Gospel of John. John, in sharp contrast to the first three Gospels, replaces the individual sayings of Jesus with long, edited discourses. Deuteronomy, also differing sharply from the rest of the Pentateuch, is constructed as a long address of Moses. In both instances, this literary form indicates deeper theological reflection.

In the sayings and narratives of the Gospels we found the non-theological language of everyday life. Israel's early traditions also concerned the everyday life of farmers and shepherds. It is taken for granted that God should be a part of this everyday life, and it is so presented in a natural way without ceremony. Herein lies the most striking and concrete parallel between the Gospels and Israel's early traditions. Just as the parables of Jesus all reflect some phase of everyday life which points beyond itself to the sovereign rule of God, so the narratives of Genesis make God's presence felt as they speak in a simple way of actual men in their normal situations in life. It is my contention that this parallel indicates how we should attempt to understand the Bible today—all abstract, theological interpretation of the Bible's message can in the final analysis be nothing more than an attempt to help those who read the Bible feel the reality of God in a very concrete way.

Martin Noth has compared the formation of the Pentateuch to

---

[7] Translator's Note: This is a somewhat technical term for the exposition, explanation, and interpretation of a biblical text, usually on the basis of a thorough study of the original language, background, context, literary form, and structure.

the growth of a tree [8] whose roots remain under the surface of the ground. In other words, the oral tradition underlying the Pentateuch must be clearly distinguished from the later literary development of the written record. This assembling or molding together of the old oral traditions was, however, a tremendous accomplishment. As a result of generations of research we now can follow, in a general way, the process by which this took place.

In the Pentateuch, however, we first had to uncover the stage at which the various independent written accounts simply existed side by side. These individual accounts are known as the Yahwist (J) account, the Elohist (E) account (according to their various uses of the names for God), and the priestly (P) account (because it presents a distinctly priestly tradition). Each of these accounts is again, in itself, an extremely complicated work. At the heart of each stands the deliverance of the Israelites out of Egypt. This is followed by the wandering in the wilderness and the entry into the Promised Land. To this was added the Sinai tradition dealing with the revelation of God and the formation of the covenant at Mount Sinai, including the proclamation of the commandments.

At this point the priestly account has added a comprehensive collection of ritual law as it had developed over a long period of time. The early history of the Israelites, as related in the patriarchal narratives of Genesis 12 through 50, was added later as a preface to these core events. As a further preface, we have the addition of the primeval history, presented along universal lines and showing how the insignificant Israelites as the people of God became part of the broad horizon of world history and of the creation of heaven and earth.

---

[8] Martin Noth, *Überlieferungsgeschichte des Pentateuch* (Stuttgart: Kohlhammer, 1948), pp. 1 and 48.

Chapter VII

Miracles in the Bible

The Bible is especially controversial with regard to the miracle stories it contains. This is understandable when one considers the fact that various periods of human history differ sharply in their experience and estimation of miracles. The fact cannot be denied that a person with no knowledge of the laws and relationships of natural science will experience and accept a miracle quite differently from someone whose understanding of the world is based on these laws and relationships. When we reflect upon the miracles in the Bible, it is important to realize that those who hear a saying are always considered part of that saying; anyone who is affected by an event becomes part of that event. Thus, the miracles, too, can be understood only within the context in which they originally occurred.

Of equal importance is the fact that the miracles are an essential part of the message of the Bible. More than one fanatic of reason has attempted to strike everything miraculous from the pages of the Bible, or at least to explain it in a natural way. But what then remains of the Bible is certainly not worth the effort of such purgative action. The Bible without miracles would simply be boring. We must, therefore, follow another, more difficult path in our attempt to understand what the miracles in the Bible actually are and what they really mean.

The German word *Wunder* is formed from a verb root. This also is true of most of the words for "wonder" found in other related

languages,[1] as well as in the language of the Bible. One cannot separate a "wonder" from the experience of that wonder; wonder can
exist only as event, never as fact. What the Bible understands by the
term "wonder" is illustrated by a passage from the Psalms, a passage
which clearly reflects the reality of wonder:

> *I will call to mind the deeds of the Lord;*
> *yea, I will remember thy wonders of old.*
> *I will meditate on all thy work,*
> *and muse on thy mighty deeds.*
> *Thy way, O God, is holy.*
> *What god is great like our God?*
> *Thou art the God who workest wonders,*
> *who hast manifested thy might among the peoples.*
> *Thou didst with thy arm redeem thy people,*
> *the sons of Jacob and Joseph.*
> *When the waters saw thee, O God,*
> *when the waters saw thee, they were afraid,*
> *yea, the deep trembled.*
> *The clouds poured out water;*
> *the skies gave forth thunder;*
> *the arrows flashed on every side.*
> *The crash of thy thunder was in the whirlwind;*
> *thy lightnings lighted up the world;*
> *the earth trembled and shook.*
> *Thy way was through the sea,*
> *thy path through the great waters;*
> *yet thy footprints were unseen.*

(Psalm 77:11-19)

It is difficult to escape the impact of such a moving account of
God's wondrous works. Only one thing can be disputed here: Is
what is here so definitely perceived as one of God's wonders really
the same as what we understand as a wonder? In this instance, such
disputing would lead us nowhere, for whoever sang this psalm made
it quite explicit: "yet thy footprints were unseen." It is the essence
of this wonder that, as an act of God, it no longer can be proved. No
traces remain to make this possible.

The controversy over miracles which has continued since the

---

[1] Translator's Note: The same is the case with the English word "wonder,"
which in this context is more accurate than "miracle" as a rendering of the
German *Wunder*.

Enlightenment [2] has completely overlooked what the Bible really means when it speaks of the miracles of God. The same is true of the church's defense of miracles; insofar as the church has defended the concrete evidence or what could be proved by concrete evidence, it really has not defended God's miracles at all. There is no way to speak of the miracles of God except as they are spoken of in this psalm—in astounding wonderment.

The miracle to which the psalmist refers is the miracle of the deliverance of the Israelites at the Reed Sea during the Exodus from Egypt. For the psalmist this event lies several centuries in the past; he no longer can experience its immediate impact. He is moved, affected, and gripped by this miracle only because he is part of the history which began with this event, not because the event, as such, happened to be so unique and magnificent, for this it apparently was not. It seems to have caused only the slightest ripple on the world scene of that day. Thus far scholars have found no historical references to it outside of the Bible, not even in such places as on the Egyptian monuments.[3] The miraculous rests in the fact that God saw fit to use this otherwise insignificant event to save this hapless band of Hebrews from slavery and thereby to reveal himself as their God and call them his people. Thus the presence of God and not the physical dimensions of the event itself makes this an occurrence of miraculous proportions.

The oldest Old Testament record of this event is found in a hymn of praise (Ex. 15:21). Near this passage there is a prose account which indicates another essential characteristic of miracle stories in the Bible (Ex. 14). Here we are not dealing with a unified account but with an account which has grown out of various layers of tradition. In the earliest layer, the event is explained simply and

---

[2] An eighteenth century movement questioning traditional values and doctrines while placing great emphasis upon the ability of man's reason to solve all his problems and answer all his questions.

[3] Translator's Note: Some biblical historians disagree on this point, citing archeological and other historical evidence which they believe refers directly to Joseph, to the stay of the Hebrews in Egypt, to the plagues and to the Hebrews' flight from Egypt. This is a matter of historical interpretation, however. The movement of the Hebrews into Egypt and out again during the Exodus does fit into the pattern of the movement of many of the Semitic peoples of that time, and there is evidence of certain natural phenomena which might relate to the Exodus. Some students consider this as historical support for the biblical account of the Exodus.

straightforwardly: "The Lord drove the sea back by a strong east wind all night, and made the sea dry land" (Ex. 14:21). In this account the miracle lies in the fact that nature suddenly interceded, spelling for the fleeing masses deliverance in the face of certain destruction. In later strata of tradition the same event is presented as being much more miraculous.

Such subsequent intensification or elevation of a miracle is common in the Bible. The same thing is found in New Testament accounts of Jesus' miracles. Precisely at this point we must acknowledge the human side of the Bible, if the miracles are to be understood and taken seriously. There is not one infallible record of a miracle in the Bible. We learn of these miracles only through *witnesses* who were confronted and moved by them. These witnesses were men who were not immune from the all-too-human tendency to exaggerate and elevate the miraculous. If we acknowledge that biblical miracle stories also were not unaffected by this tendency, we no longer will need to cling anxiously to concrete evidence of these miracles. Instead, we will feel free to discuss and reflect on them in a positive manner.

This is beautifully expressed in that passage from the Psalms to which we just referred. Reflecting upon God's great acts of the past, the psalmist was compelled to cry out, "Thou art the God who workest wonders," thereby opening the way for his future discussion of God's miracles. Thus the third essential characteristic of biblical miracles makes its appearance: Because the miraculous is an integral part of God's sovereign rule, his miracles range from the most insignificant trifle to the most stupendous event. God's people in community experience his miracles as they make their way through history, and the miraculous is there for each individual to experience as he makes his way through life. The birth of a child is considered just as miraculous as deliverance from a deadly peril: the quieting of hunger pangs is no less a miracle than the coming of a Redeemer.

All of life is filled with miracles; there are no areas, nooks, or crannies, no stretches along the way, where a miracle cannot occur. That the miracles are works of God is demonstrated precisely by the fact that their magnitude can never be measured by the external phenomena which accompany them. The most insignificant and natural occurrence can awaken just as much jubilation over

God's wonders as can something which is entirely out of the ordinary, something which never has occurred before.

It is understandable that our perception of the real essence of the biblical miracle should be clouded. We have become accustomed to viewing New Testament miracles objectively, at a distance, as an isolated fact of the past, and all this under the question of whether they actually happened as they are reported, or whether they happened a bit differently, or perhaps not at all. But these are basically questions which seek external evidence left behind by the miracles; they are not questions about the miracles themselves. We have accustomed ourselves to limiting the material-physical side of Jesus' miracles to the time of his ministry; this side of his miracles no longer reaches us today. However, if one of these stories in which Jesus heals a sick person, stills a storm, or returns a child to his mother does not bring from us the jubilant outburst of the psalmist, "Thou art the God who workest wonders," if we view it only in retrospect, then it also will make little difference how much of the story we consider to be true. To preach today on these miracle stories can have meaning only if they involve us in that history which began with the words and deeds of Jesus. But in so doing we must remember that the material-physical side of Jesus' ministry was also a part of all this and still is today. It cannot simply be eliminated by some spiritual reinterpretation.

We will arrive again at a forward-directed proclamation of the miracles if we free ourselves of this obsession with the external evidence and if we expect God to work his miracles in our changed world in a manner quite different from the manner in which he performed them during the time of Jesus. For example, the use of medical science and technical skill in healing a child of an apparently fatal disease can be understood by his parents as a miracle from the hand of God in the same way that Jairus and his wife (Mark 5:21-43) viewed Jesus' healing of their child as one of God's miracles.

The Bible can also speak critically of miracles. In Jesus' own words, the statement about faith to move mountains is paralleled by the warning against an obsession with miracles. He flatly rejects the Pharisees' demands for miracles (Mark 8:11-13). He expresses the same feelings in his answer to doubting Thomas (John 20:29). Here the Bible's criticism of miracle-faith and miracle-seeking best illustrates the fact that the Bible's concern is not with the external evidence of a miracle, but with the working of God in that miracle. The miracle remains the special work of God; it does not attempt to become commonplace. Where there is too much talk of God's miracles, the impact of these miracles can be destroyed. Again, the Old Testament clearly illustrates this fact. During some periods of Israel's history many signs and wonders are performed, as during the period of the wandering in the wilderness. During other periods one cannot find the slightest trace of a miracle. Instead, the working of God is awesomely affirmed in the normal course of events, the cause and effect of which are plainly visible, as in the narrative of David's succession to the throne.

A sense of wonderment must be part of every experience of a miracle, and in the Psalms this sense of wonderment is an important element in the praise of God. Children are best at expressing wonderment. In all wonderment there remains an element of childlikeness. Our world has become extremely sophisticated; the farther we progress in our mastery of the world and its elements, the more we push this childlikeness to the fringe of our technological existence. Yet it would be senseless to try to stop progress, for the miracles referred to in the Bible are also far ahead of our times. It would be of more value to approach our changed world as though we expected miracles to happen and then to be prepared to accept them with a sense of awe and wonderment. What value would there be in a life without miracles, and what would it profit a man if he gained the whole world and could no longer stand in awe and wonderment?

Chapter VIII

Feeding the Multitude

Twentieth century man reads the story of the feeding of the four thousand, as recorded in Chapter 15 of Matthew's Gospel:

> And they all ate and were satisfied; and they took up seven baskets full of the broken pieces left over. Those who ate were four thousand men, besides women and children.

He asks, openly or silently, "Did it really happen this way?" How should we imagine that it did happen? Did Jesus make the bread out of nothing? How did all this actually take place? More important than the answers is the fact that such questions must be faced by those who accept the story as it stands, as well as by those who cannot believe that out of nothing Jesus could have made bread for four thousand persons.

How did it take place, *how* was it possible that suddenly there was enough bread for so many people? In our western way of thinking, everything depends on this "how." For us this determines whether or not the story is true. However, by limiting ourselves to the question of "how," we do not hear the story as it was intended by those who recorded it for us. Only in passing do we notice that the story did not take place within the context of our concept of natural law, or that the writer was not presenting an act of Jesus which had occurred in opposition to the laws of nature.

If we want to understand the story as it was intended to be understood, we should not place it into the context of a natural event (that is, as occurring in direct opposition to the laws of nature) but into the context of history. Those persons in whose presence this miracle was performed, and who reported it to others, lived in the world of the Old Testament. It is their history that is related in the Old Testament, and in this history another miracle of feeding enjoys a central position: the miraculous feeding with manna in the wilderness. This feeding belongs among the redemptive gifts associated with the saving act of God which formed the basis for the covenant. There the story stands, a constant reminder that God has possibilities for feeding his hungry children where they themselves no longer can see any possibility of silencing the pangs of their hunger.

In reading the account in Exodus 16, it becomes evident that a whole series of extensions, inferences, reflections, and deductions gradually became entwined around what originally was a brief and simple story of the wonderful feeding in the wilderness. This reaches the point where the priestly account even connects the story with the Sabbath, adding in a legendary fashion how the bread which had been gathered on the sixth day lasted also for the seventh, the Sabbath. Or, it is pointed out that regardless of how much or how little each gathered, it was always the right amount: "he that gathered much had nothing over, and he that gathered little had no lack, each had gathered according to what he could eat." A later reflection on the story is the comment that no one should keep any of this wonderful food for the next morning, and if extra food were kept, it would be destroyed; for a concern about the morrow had nothing to do with this food.

It is clear what direction was taken by the ideas which attached themselves to this old story as it was handed down. The miracle was not the appearance of the food—which was explained quite naturally: "it was like coriander seed, white, and the taste of it was like wafers made with honey." The miracle lay more in the fact that in the moment of greatest need God found a completely unexpected way to satisfy the hunger of his people. All further reflection on the event was for the sole purpose of explaining what the miracle meant for the people. What was really important was the fact that each received enough, that each received it quite simply and without concern for the coming day, that the manna gave indication of God's possibilities and thus silenced the murmuring of the people.

This redemptive gift had been given to the people on their way to the Promised Land, a land which had been described as flowing with milk and honey. When the Israelites arrived in the land, ate of its fruit, and enjoyed the blessings of its fields, the story of the bread in the wilderness was to live on in the experience of young and old alike: "And you shall remember all the way which the Lord your God has led you these forty years in the wilderness. . . . he humbled you and let you hunger and fed you with manna, which you did not know, nor did your fathers know; that he might make you know that man does not live by bread alone, but that man lives by everything that proceeds out of the mouth of the Lord" (Deut. 8:2-3). This word from Deuteronomy, which sounds like a sermon on the feeding in the wilderness, indicates in a beautiful and living way how this event lived on.

Thus, from the Old Testament we get a clear outline of the broader and deeper context to which the feeding of the four thousand belongs. The former question of "how" suddenly seems trifling and unimportant. If this took place in an entirely natural way, as in the case of the manna in the wilderness, the story loses none of its meaning. For is it really so important that we know this? Can we not stop where the story stops, where it has no more to say? It is also irrelevant whether such a wonderful feeding occurred once or several times—it is transmitted to us six times in the Gospels—or how many were fed, for the number could have grown during the transmission of the story, as so often occurred.

Now we should be able to hear what this story actually attempts to tell us. Jesus said to his disciples, "I have compassion on the crowd . . . they have nothing to eat." This was the statement of one who was truly a man among men, who had experienced hunger himself. This hunger was one of the reasons for his coming, and he possessed the power to satisfy it. In him and in those gathered around him we have a continuation of what God's people of old had known: that whoever takes God seriously in his life and trusts him will not only recognize the bread of blessing which he eats every day, for which he works, and of which the psalmist says, "The eyes of all look to thee, and thou givest them their food in due season" (Psalm 145:15). He also will recognize the bread of deliverance or preservation for which he has done nothing and which comes to him as a miracle.

In the Gospels' account of the wonderful feeding, this bread of preservation was incorporated into the story of Jesus of Nazareth. This Jesus really cannot be understood or fully accepted so long as one ignores his compassion for physical hunger and attempts to make faith in him a strictly spiritual experience. For the hungry as for the well-fed it is important to see the connection between the bread they possess, or for which they hunger, and the God who can use this bread to perform miracles. In a time when the production of daily bread has become a human undertaking of great proportions, this biblical statement about the bread of preservation beside the bread of blessing assumes a significance it has never assumed before. With the threatening world population explosion, the significance of this statement will once again speak to us in a dynamic way. Even with the most vigorous economic endeavors to assure an adequate supply of daily bread, there never will be an oversupply of the bread of preservation as long as the earth exists. Were the Bible ever to cease its proclamation of the miracles of feeding in time of greatest need, were it no longer to speak of God's mercy toward those in hunger, or the joy of those who receive this bread of preservation, then something of the humanness of mankind would be lost.

I was once told by a man who had returned from a Siberian concentration camp that in his unit the sign of the cross was made over every piece of food which was received. In this unit there were persons from all nations, and not one was a Christian. But someone had started the practice, and they all joined in. To them this was a sign that the food was more than just food.

The miraculous feeding of the multitude opens for us a still broader horizon. In the Gospel of John, Jesus says concerning himself, "I am the Bread of Life" (John 6:35, 48). We are usually quick to interpret such a statement in a strictly figurative sense and to associate it with elevated ideas which are far removed from the concrete reality of daily bread. But we should note that this statement follows the account of the feeding of the multitude, as well as the entire series of bread miracles which runs through the Bible, from the manna in the wilderness to the bread which the ravens brought to Elijah (1 Kings 7:4-6), to the many deliverances from hunger reflected in the Psalms. Thus Jesus is here associating daily bread inseparably with the activity of God.

Against this background one now can make the statement that Jesus himself was the essential, the real, the all-embracing miracle of God, and that all the miracles Jesus performed point to that miracle which he himself was. The miracle here does not rest in what one can see of Jesus, or through him, but entirely upon what one experiences as he is confronted by Jesus.

Once, near the end of his ministry, Jesus directed this question to his disciples: "When I sent you out with no purse or bag or sandals, did you lack anything?" And the disciples answered, "Nothing" (Luke 22:35). This was not a direct reference to the miracles of feeding, but it was a reference to the bread of preservation which Jesus' disciples had experienced while in his service. This realization that even the stilling of one's hunger pangs can be understood as a miracle bestows upon daily bread a certain dignity which comes with the realization that through daily bread we can be brought into relationship with God.

Here, then, is the link between the disciples' answer to Jesus' question, "Did you lack anything?" and the miracles of feeding, as well as the meals which were part of Jesus' fellowship with his disciples, and, beyond this, the accounts of the institution of the Last Supper. In this broad and comprehensive sense we hear Jesus say: "I am the Bread of Life."

Chapter IX

Stilling the Storm

Among the miracle stories of the Bible, the story of the stilling of the storm has a strikingly lonely place. This is the only instance where we find Jesus helping his disciples in a situation where their lives were endangered. What was the reason for preserving this story and what did it say to those who heard it?

At the very heart of the story we hear a cry of distress: "Save, Lord; we are perishing" (Matt. 8:25). This cry for help has the dimensions of everything human. Wherever men exist, they know the life-threatening eruptions of the elements, the fear of death, and the cry for help.

In this respect, the story of the stilling of the storm points out something essential to the biblical narratives: It speaks as a story, by itself, without further commentary. There is really nothing further to explain about the raging of the elements, about the disciples in their boat struggling for their lives, or about their experience of deliverance. Anyone who has experienced life as it really is knows all this and recognizes it.

But to those who originally heard this story, and to those who passed it on, this cry for help was more than the cry of all men experiencing the fear of death. For each of these hearers this cry touched on part of their own history. At the beginning of their history an entire epoch resounded with this cry. As in no other later period, the period of the wandering in the wilderness was marked by the powerful rhythm of distress and deliverance. God's people moved from one danger to another in a precipitous up-and-down movement of anxiety and jubilation, from the sharp cry of distress to the relaxed sigh of relief. The remembrance of this epoch was never completely blotted out, and it was immediately awakened whenever a similar situation arose. Even if the storm on the Sea of Galilee was not a major, earth-shaking event, for the men whose ship was seized by the storm, whose lives were threatened, something which had happened in the early history of their people became their own experience.

Only in this light can we begin to understand one of the most obvious features of the story—the fact that in the midst of the raging storm, one among them slept. This shows that Jesus could not be threatened by the storm, that he was secure in the hands of the Father. It is of equal importance that through Jesus' sleeping in the midst of the storm the disciples came to the realization that their Master did not appear endangered by what was to them a major peril. The possibility that the ship might sink did not seem to disturb him at all. "Do you not care if we perish?" they asked (Mark 4:38). In this accusing question we again have the situation which existed at the beginning of the history of God's people. There too, in the face of so many deadly perils, such a question had been directed at their mediator.

This threat to the disciples did not seem to bother Jesus. The disciples had noticed this on other occasions, and they could not understand it. One of them summarized the entire ministry of Jesus with these words: "But we had hoped that he was the one to redeem Israel" (Luke 24:21). This indicates how difficult it was for the disciples to understand Jesus' true mission; they could not understand that instead of destroying the hostile forces with an act of deliverance, he slept while the others struggled for rescue.

But the story does not stop here. Jesus himself was present in the ship. He was a man and thus also truly endangered. He allowed himself to be awakened, rebuked the waves, and they became still. Thus, Jesus shared the omnipotence of God and was able to command the threatening elements when it was his hour.

This is why the event was passed on, why it became an essential part of the message of the Gospels. The story of the storm affirms the fact that in the activity of Jesus we have a continuation of what had been the keynote of Israel's early history—God's wonderful deliverance in times of grave distress when the life of the community was threatened.

This story of the storm also has been interpreted as having reference to the ship of the church which through the storms of time is preserved by her Lord. Such an interpretation would not violate the story, but its essential purpose was to show how all ordinary men, even believers, are exposed to the constant threats of the erupting elements, experience fear and cry out for help. In the strictest sense, the activity of Jesus and the message he brought had nothing to do with the eruption and recession of the storm or the frailty of the ship. Instead, the story attempts to show that in these situations Christ is near his own and majestically brings to bear the hidden omnipotence at his disposal as evidence of the fact that he is our Savior, even in the elemental emergencies of our human existence.

Just as this story stands alone among many other stories which are quite different from it, so also the experience of what Christ performed there never will become commonplace. What is commonplace is the experience that Christ's power does *not* manifest itself to everyone—that he appears to be sleeping. Here we are reminded of the Psalm of Lament in the Old Testament, where with directness and simplicity the psalmist cries to God: "Rouse thyself! . . . Awake! . . . Rise up . . . " (Psalm 44:23, 26).

The story of the storm is closely related to the story of Jesus' walking on the water (Mark 6:45-52). The situation was the same: A storm on the Sea of Galilee threw the disciples into distress. The purpose is also the same: Jesus stills the storm. What is different is the fact that instead of being in the boat, Jesus was on the shore. He became aware of the distress of the men at sea; and "about the fourth watch of the night he came to them, walking on the sea." The disciples thought they saw a ghost and became terrified until they recognized Jesus as he spoke to them. Then he got into the boat with them, and the wind ceased. In the Gospel of Matthew this is followed by the episode of Peter's sinking as he, too, attempted to walk on the water (Matt. 14:22-33).

When one compares the story of Jesus' walking on the water with the story of the stilling of the storm, it becomes apparent that this story possesses the character of a narrative which has been edited and pieced together. It does not have a definitely closed, lucid, and rounded character like the story of the stilling of the storm. When one underlines those features which are common to both, what then remains comprises an occurrence which is complete in itself and could be related apart from the story of the stilling of the storm. In Jesus' walking on the water, the disciples experienced an epiphany, a manifestation of a divine being, and were terrified by it; Jesus then identified himself with the words which had been spoken since ancient times by God or an angel when they made their appearances, "Fear not, I am . . . . " [1] These two originally independent stories are here bound together by the motif of the walking on the water.

When one reads the account of this second event, detached from the account of the stilling of the storm, it seems unusual that such a manifestation should have its place here, the midpoint in Jesus' earthly life, especially since he had been together with his disciples just prior to this. It has been assumed that behind this story there stands the account of an appearance of the resurrected Christ before his disciples, and that this story was later incorporated into the account of the stilling of the storm. This assumption is further supported by the fact that the words Jesus spoke were strikingly similar to the words found in the resurrection narratives.

In any event, the story of Jesus' walking on the water, as we now have it, is an intensification of the account of the stilling of the storm. This tendency to intensify by means of expansion can be followed still further in the episode of Peter's sinking, which has been added by Matthew (Matt. 14:22-33). Here it is plain how the disciples' cry for help is no longer merely a cry for help in time of elemental need; it is now the believer's cry for help as his faith wavers, the cry of the doubter who because of his doubt has fallen into danger. A further intensification of the miraculous is shown in John's account of the same story of Jesus' walking on the water (John 6:16-21). There the boat immediately arrives at the shore after Jesus enters it, and all danger is past.

We can see from these expansions that we are dealing with a later stage in the development of the tradition. The miraculous is intensified, altering somewhat the meaning of the event. Now Jesus is no longer the one through whom the old experience of wonderful deliverance is renewed; he is the supra-human, the otherworldly

---

[1] Cf. Gen. 15:1; 26:24. Judges 6:23, Isa. 41:10, etc.

one, who manifests himself to his disciples in his otherworldliness.

One can detect a legendary characteristic which intensified the miracle of the storm and thus expressed in a more tangible and direct manner the fact that Jesus, who was human just like his disciples, in the moment of greatest need came to them as one from another world, as one who possessed great power. We should therefore view this as testimony of the further impact upon the disciples of the stilling of the storm and as evidence of how this event was preserved, reflected upon, and modified.

In the Book of Job we find this statement concerning God "who . . . trampled the waves of the sea" (Job 9:8b). When this also is said of Jesus, we are reminded that the disciples, even as disciples of Jesus, remained vulnerable human beings exposed to all the elemental threats of life and through this experience learned that their Lord could help them in such times of danger. They experienced what is expressed so powerfully in one of the Psalms:

> *The floods have lifted up, O Lord,*
> *the floods have lifted up their voice,*
> *the floods lift up their roaring.*
> *Mightier than the thunders of many waters,*
> *mightier than the waves of the sea,*
> *the Lord on high is mighty!*

> (Psalm 93:3-4)

Chapter X

Creator and Creation

The miracles of Jesus all relate to the creation faith, which, as we shall see, involves much more than just the belief that God created heaven and earth. When Jesus healed a sick person, stilled a storm, or satisfied the hungry, he was doing something related to the activity of the Creator. The entire New Testament is based on the assumption that its listeners or readers accept the presence of God's creative activity in the world. In Romans, Chapter 1, for instance, the heathen are considered unpardonable because they have not shown their due thankfulness to God. In Romans 14 the giving of thanks expresses affirmation of the Creator. The same is true in Philippians (4:10-13) where Paul has such trust in the Creator that he can enjoy abundance and suffer want, that he can simply accept the gifts of creation as God offers them to him.

For those who speak here, as well as for their listeners, the creation faith is still unbroken; no one needs first to be convinced that God created heaven and earth. How different today! When we speak of God, we must face the fact that many people no longer accept him as the Creator but believe that the world came into being as the result of natural causes.

For this reason most of us have a false picture of what the creation faith means as we find it in the Bible. What the Bible says about the Creator and the creation must be disassociated from purely philosophical reflection. We could search through the entire Bible and not find the slightest trace of such purely abstract questions as these: Must the world be viewed as created, and why? In what relationship do creation and development stand to each other? How does the creation of the first human beings relate to what we mean by the statement, "I believe that God has created *me* . . . "? The Bible has no interest in such questions, because in biblical times no one asked them. Creation belonged to the obvious.

The Bible also does not deal with those questions which have become so important to man since the creation of the world became such a matter of controversy. These questions arise especially from the early chapters of the Bible, questions such as these: Was the world really created in seven days? What does it mean when the creation of light precedes the creation of the heavenly bodies? Was Eve really created from the rib of Adam? Did the serpent actually speak to Eve? Questions of this nature are not raised in the Bible itself and will not bring us one step closer to an understanding of the creation faith as found there.

An understanding and appreciation of the creation faith of the Bible can be gained only from the simple and grateful joy of being a creature. This joy almost incidentally breaks through, in a warm and radiant fashion, in the proclamation of Jesus:

> *"Therefore I tell you, do not be anxious about your life, what you shall eat or what you shall drink, nor about your body, what you shall put on. Is not life more than food, and the body more than clothing?*
>
> *"Look at the birds of the air: they neither sow nor reap nor gather into barns, and yet your heavenly Father feeds them. Are you not of more value than they? . . .*
>
> *"And why are you anxious about clothing?*
>
> *"Consider the lilies of the field, how they grow; they neither toil nor spin; yet I tell you, even Solomon in all his glory was not arrayed like one of these."*

(Matt. 6:25-26, 28-29)

One must view the miracles Jesus performed in direct relationship to this message. Because the heavenly Father feeds the birds of the air and clothes the lilies of the field, Jesus commands the raging storm, satisfies the hungry, and says to the sick, "Be healed!" In both instances it is a matter of the Creator's love for his creation, of his compassion for his suffering creatures, that they might be happy and rejoice in their existence.

This can be put into proper perspective when viewed against the background of the Old Testament where a mighty symphony is formed as the joy of the creature is expressed in praise of the Creator. What the biblical creation faith really means can be heard, for instance, in this passage from the Psalms:

> When I look at thy heavens, the work of thy fingers,
> The moon and the stars which thou hast established;
> what is man that thou art mindful of him,
> And the son of man that thou dost care for him?
>
> (Psalm 8:3, 4)

This viewing of the heavens is the same as the viewing of the lilies and the birds in the Sermon on the Mount. In each instance, man becomes aware of himself as a creature, and this awareness is directly related to the Creator's care of his creatures. This moving, breathless beholding of the creation has nothing to do with a theoretical retracing of the process by which this all originated. In the quotation from the Sermon on the Mount, as in this Psalm, man looks beyond the creation to the Creator, who "is mindful of *man* and cares for him."

What this faith in the Creator meant for God's people of old can be shown from another Old Testament passage where someone also pointed to the stars. This time it was the gaze of a tired and despairing people which was directed upward:

> Lift your eyes on high and see!
> Who created such things
> and brings out their host in great numbers?
> He calls them all by name;
> his might and the power of his strength are so great
> that not one can be found missing.[1]
>
> (Isa. 40:26)

That is the creation faith of the Bible! We have erred wherever we have attempted to base the creation faith on the first chapters of Genesis. These chapters serve as the introductions to two historical works: Chapter 1 introduces the priestly writing and Chapters 2 and 3 introduce the Yahwistic history. Only within the context of these two historical writings can the first chapters of Genesis be

---

[1] Translator's Note: The above translation differs from the RSV and follows the author's German version.

properly understood. It would be wrong and out of accord with the whole Bible if we were to take these isolated chapters, detached from their context, and develop a doctrine of creation without taking into account all other biblical statements on the subject.

It is for this reason that we have reached the point in recent times where the creation faith of the Bible has been thrown into an unhealthy conflict with natural science, where it has been distorted and reduced to a theory about the origin of man and the world. It is time for the church to make it clear that the fundamental creation faith of the Bible is found in the stirring, breathless praise of the Creator for his wonderful works, and that the various creation accounts always originated from this praise.

Man will never know exactly how God created the world. To point out this limitation, the men who compiled that monumental work known as the Pentateuch wisely placed two accounts of creation side by side at the very beginning. This was a warning that men should not desire to know too much. Aside from these two accounts, there are numerous other, sharply differing creation accounts in the Old Testament, especially in the Psalms. With this the Bible has made it clear that the creation *concept* has changed and could change without destroying what is essential—the praise of the Creator for his works. This praise of the Creator and joy over his creation, this trust in the goodness of him who directs the course of the sun and shows mercy toward an animal, runs through the entire Old Testament and has a much broader and deeper significance than is generally recognized.

Not only the creation psalms but every part of the Old Testament resounds with praise of the Creator. When, in the Book of Job (Job 38–39), the praise of the Creator expands into intense and colorful portrayals of plants, animals, and natural phenomena such as a thunderstorm, one senses that the Bible's unique understanding of the beautiful is being unfolded. Here beauty is not isolated into an aesthetic realm; the creature is beautiful as creator and he is beautiful in relationship to God. Beauty is not first of all something that is but something that happens.

At the end of the creation story we read, " . . . and behold, it was very good" (Gen. 1:31). To fully understand this, we must also hear the statement "it was very beautiful." This beauty of the creation is event insofar as the creation itself is called forth to praise God:

"Praise him, you highest heavens . . . and all deeps, fire and hail, snow and frost, stormy wind fulfilling his command!" (Psalm 148:4a, 7b, 8)

In a world in which man largely treats the rest of creation as the material and energy he is untiringly attempting to control to use in his own advancement, this biblical conception of the created order should give us something to think about. According to this biblical conception, every part of the created order has a value in itself; it can never become simply material—matter—because in the final analysis it is creature, just like man and, like man, finds its ultimate meaning in its relationship to the Creator. This biblical conception also gives to art a great significance, insofar as individual works of art give expression to this beauty reflected in the created order.

Once again we return to the miracles of Jesus which stand in closest relationship to the creative activity of God. From those who witnessed one of his miracles we hear these words like an echo: "He has done all things well; he even makes the deaf hear and the dumb speak" (Mark 7:37, Isa. 35:5). Here we can observe the relationship of Jesus' activity to the creative activity of God as a sentence from the praises of the Creator is used to express wonder over Jesus' miracle and joy over the fact that in Christ the day of salvation has dawned. The unity of the Testaments also signifies the unity of the Creator and the Redeemer. The same God who sent his Son to redeem mankind also clothes the lilies of the field.

Chapter XI

Beginning and End of History

Is the Bible really able to provide information about the beginning and the end of history? During recent decades this question has been raised from many different standpoints. The answer, although controversial, is especially important today in view of the possibility that man himself possesses the means to bring an end to world history.

The creation narratives at the beginning of the Bible can be understood only as introductions to those two historical works which describe in broad outline Israel's history from the beginning to their own time. How can any people trace its history back to the creation of the world? Can we classify this as history at all? Here is where the criticism begins. History, according to our understanding, cannot begin until there are objective and verifiable historical sources or documents, and there can be no documents dealing with the creation. This historical objection is entirely justified.

When the creation narratives at the beginning of the Bible are viewed as historical documents, they are misunderstood. They also were never intended to be revelations about the beginning of the world. If this were the case, it would not be comprehensible why the Bible should contain differing accounts of this event. These narratives do not testify to history, but to the extension of God's activity, which Israel had experienced in her own history, to the entire universe. The statement that God created heaven and earth is a statement of praise to the Creator.

55

In their present position at the beginning of the works describing Israel's history, these creation chapters serve to portray this relatively minor series of events against the broadest conceivable horizon and thereby to express its essential meaning. Israel's history itself has a much broader meaning, because God has chosen it to be the arena of his activity. With the command to depart from his homeland, Abraham received the promise, "In you all the families of the earth will be blessed" (Gen. 12:3).[1] It is for this reason that, preceding this promise, the first chapters of the Bible speak of the generations of the earth as a whole, of the origins of the world and of the human race. Israel's history is viewed against the background of the beginning of world history because Israel did not exist for herself alone. Her history, as God's history with his people, is part of a much broader picture.

To do justice to the Bible's affirmations about the beginning of history, it is important to inquire as to how these affirmations were arrived at. In the earliest traditions it is simply the beginning of Israel's history: God's saving act brought into existence a people, and that was considered to be the beginning. In reality, however, this was only the beginning of an ethnic group, the Israelites. But in this early period the individual person was so completely a member of the group, the group was his world to such an extent, that he never inquired beyond it about any other beginning, either of man or of the world.

The next step involves the question of the beginning of the human race. This question stands at the heart of the earliest creation narrative in Genesis 2 and 3.[2] It did not arise, however, as a question about the origin of man but rather as a question about the perplexing nature of human existence which presses upon man in the face of death. Why is man as he is? Why does he blossom

---

[1] Translator's Note: Here the RSV reads "*by* you all the families of the earth *will bless themselves*."

[2] Translator's Note: As is here indicated, the two creation accounts at the beginning of the Bible are generally considered to have originated in different periods of Israel's history. The earlier account in Genesis 2 and 3 probably took form around the time of David and Solomon, during the ninth or perhaps even tenth century b.c. It has been attributed to the "J" writer. The later account in Genesis 1 probably originated shortly before or after the end of the Exile (sixth or fifth century b.c.) and is part of the "Priestly" tradition. Cf. Chapter 6 above, esp. p. 33.

forth only to wither? From this question we can hardly disassociate the questions of suffering and guilt which are of ultimate concern in this earliest of the two creation accounts. In other words, the question concerning the beginning of human existence is at the same time the question concerning its meaning, and seldom has this question been raised in such a profound and comprehensive manner as here. This account of the beginning presents its answer in terms of faith in the Creator who has something other than death in mind for man, who forgives those who have sinned, and who gives to mortal existence a meaning which, even in its fallen state, binds it to the Creator.

It is in the third step in this inquiry that we first encounter something which somewhat corresponds to our approach to the beginning. The later creation narrative in Genesis 1 inquires about the origin of the universe. But even in this third stage there is no universe in our sense, no world which exists of and for itself. The creation of the world has man as its goal, and man, in turn, is not a part of nature but is viewed in relation to God, is created in the image of God, and it is not possible to separate the created from the Creator, to understand it by itself, as Nature. Old Testament man expanded his world view from the innermost circle of this little wandering group to the broadest circumference of all things. Out of the overwhelming awareness of the ever-broadening dimensions of God's sovereign rule, out of the extolling of his ever-expanding activity, the arch was cast from God, the Deliverer of his people, to God, the Creator of heaven and earth.

In the New Testament the discussion of the end of the world serves the same purpose as this Old Testament tracing of the beginning of history back to the beginning of all creation. Here, also, the central act of God, the Christ-Event, is linked with world history. In the coming of Christ something of significance for the world took place. The statement from the Gospel of John, "For God so loved *the world* that he gave his only begotten Son [3] . . . ," is an exact parallel to the promise to Abraham, through whom all the families of the earth would be blessed. Therefore, throughout the entire New Testament the coming of salvation in Christ is connected with the end of the world. This becomes apparent in the

---

[3] Translator's Note: Here the RSV translation of John 3:16 reads "only Son."

Gospels' statements about the coming of the kingdom, the Day of Judgment, and the return of Christ. It appears again and again in the letters of the apostles, and finally it is spelled out in detail in the Revelation to John.

In the New Testament the discussion of the end of the world is conducted no differently than the discussion of the beginning of the world in the Old Testament. Here as there, the essential factor is that the history of salvation, which must run its course within a limited area and period of time, is brought into relationship to the entire course of history. In the old covenant, when the people of God no longer could find any meaning in their own history, they were directed to the stars and to their Creator. In the new covenant the congregation or the individual Christian is told that at the end of the world, which still is hidden, stands Christ. The statements concerning the beginning and the end always receive their meaning only from the present into which they were spoken.

Herein lie the boundaries of the biblical discussion concerning the beginning and the end. We have said that it is not possible to derive from the first creation chapters of the Bible an objective, valid account of the origin of the world. Exactly the same thing applies to the descriptions of the end of the world in the New Testament, not only in the more detailed description in the Revelation to John but also in the shorter descriptions in the Gospels (Mark 13, etc.) and in the Epistles. This is not just a recent consideration; the inclusion of the Revelation to John in the New Testament was seriously questioned for a long time by major segments of Christianity. At one point in the New Testament itself, statements concerning the end become quite divergent.

From the generation of Jesus and his disciples until the time the New Testament writings received their final form, a significant change took place regarding the end. The first generation anticipated the end of the world to be imminent and with it the return of Christ in glory. The next generation had to come to terms with the delay in Christ's return; this is especially clear from Paul's Epistles. This is further pointed out in Chapter 5 of John's Gospel where two statements stand side by side, one stating that for those who believe in Christ the judgment already has been overcome, and the other stating that the hour still is coming when the dead will come forth from their graves to the resurrection of life or to the resurrection of judgment (John 5:24-29).

The groundwork for this was laid in the Old Testament. The promise to Abraham, "In you all the families of the earth will be blessed" (Gen. 12:3), was not fulfilled throughout the entire history recorded in the Old Testament. Rather, Israel's significance in world history diminished. The promise given to the house of David became a reality and lasted for several centuries, but then the kingdom fell apart and the promise to David lived on as an unfulfilled promise. It was out of this soil that the apocalyptic writings arose, that is, revelations concerning the future judgment of the world and the dawn of the new age of salvation. An abundance of such "revelations" appeared during the centuries around the birth of Christ, only a few of which were included in the Bible—Daniel and the little apocalypse of Isaiah 24-27 in the Old Testament and the Revelation to John in the New Testament. Now, through the Dead Sea scrolls, we have new information about the apocalyptic literature. We now realize that it enjoyed a significance which we can hardly imagine, but these writings were never confirmed by history.

How was it possible that unfulfilled promises could be passed on for such a long period of time and be treasured by a believing community even though history continued untouched by them? What does it signify when throughout entire generations work was carried on with glowing devotion toward the development of outlines or sketches of the end of the world, the result of which had such a resounding effect that they gained entrance into both the Old and the New Testament?

One can at least sense an answer in the following statements from a book by Karl Löwith:

> The significance of this vision of an ultimate end . . . is that it provides a scheme of progressive order and meaning, a scheme which has been capable of overcoming the ancient fear of fate and fortune. Not only does the *eschaton* delimit the process of history by an end, it also articulates and fulfills it by a definite goal. . . . Comparable to the compass which gives us orientation in space, and thus enables us to conquer it, the eschatological compass gives orientation in time by pointing to the King-

dom of God as the ultimate end and purpose. It is also only within this . . . eschatological scheme of the historical process that history became "universal" . . . .[4]

These statements illustrate the fact that the Bible does not intend that we should develop for ourselves a picture of the beginning or the end. We simply do not know either the beginning or the end, even from the Bible. The Bible's concern is, rather, that we understand history as coming from God and leading to God, that our world and its history have a meaning which can be affirmed by faith from any point in this history, a meaning which can unite every man with this whole.

Therefore there is profound significance in the fact that the Bible as we read it today depicts a history which begins with the creation of all things and closes with the end of the world, thereby relating every period of history and every man in his place in history to that One referred to by the psalmist:

Lord, thou hast been our dwelling place in all generations
Before the mountains were brought forth,
or ever thou hadst formed the earth and the world,
from everlasting to everlasting thou art God.

(Psalm 90:1-2)

---

[4] Karl Löwith, *Meaning in History* (Chicago: The University of Chicago Press, 1949), p. 18.

Chapter XII

The Bible and the Word of God

Thus far we have discussed the two broad horizons contained in the message of the Bible, creation and history, everything that has been created and everything that has occurred. At the heart of these two great entities stands the Word of God. "Word of God" has become such a common and often carelessly used concept that it requires special attention.

Word of God—that is a contradiction in itself, for to say that God can speak is to conceive of him as being human. For this reason there always have been passionate disputes over the alleged superstition that God can speak and that man can hear his words. From this we can conclude that the Word of God cannot be extracted from the Bible as easily as is often thought. As an example, at more than one point in the Bible God's Word stands in opposition to God's Word. This is true in the history of prophecy and in the controversies of Jesus. In other words, the Word of God in the Bible is not a smooth and simple unity; it is more often hidden beneath contradictions, obscurities, and difficult questions. This, again, is based on the fact that the Word of God is essentially an impossibility because it would confine God within the limits of a human concept.

Respect for this mystery must be the starting point of any reflection upon the Word of God. Whenever we say "Word of God" we are speaking of what is essentially incomprehensible and impossible; we are saying that God is involved in time, in temporal-historical

61

reality, which, however, cannot contain or comprehend him; we are speaking of a miracle.

In the history of biblical interpretation there has always existed a highly conservative and a highly critical emphasis. Everyone usually is convinced that the conservative emphasis originates from a more reverent attitude than does the critical emphasis. But is that so certain? Is it not possible that in a strictly conservative interpretation there lurks the danger that the hidden quality of God's Word, the inconceivable miracle that we can ever speak of such a thing, will recede too much into the background, behind the certainty that we possess it, that we have control over it?

The prologue to the Gospel of John (John 1:1-18), at the very heart of the Bible, speaks of this miracle of God's Word. The one who is speaking here is especially conscious of this mystery. From these forceful words we can learn anew to speak more reverently and cautiously concerning the Word of God. Here the concept that through his Word the supernatural God touches our earthly existence is given fullest expression:

The Word became flesh and dwelt among us.
(John 1:14)

We also could express it in this way: The Word became history and shared in the reality of our existence. What is described in this statement is nothing more than a paraphrase, a stronger description of the concept "Word of God." What is described here actually took place with each word that God spoke to a human being. In each instance, God's Word became history and shared in the reality of our human existence. Each word that God ever spoke portrayed this miracle and therefore can also be disputed, denied, and questioned.

Furthermore, the prologue of John tells us that the Word of God now, at this one point in human history, became human and dwelt among us as a human being. This occurrence is placed against the broad horizon of creation and history. At the beginning of the prologue, the Word is related to the creation: "In the beginning was the Word . . . and all things were created through the same." [1]

This statement directly resumes what the Old Testament creation

---

[1] Translator's Note: Here the RSV reads "through him."

account had brought to such forceful expression as it introduced each act of creation with the phrase—"And God said . . . " (Gen. 1). Therefore, wherever a word of God becomes perceptible, he who created the heavens and the earth will also be perceived. There can be no Word of God which does not point to the beginning and thus to the all-inclusive, creative activity of God.

John's prologue now takes this a step farther as it relates the Word of God to the concepts of light and life which embrace all existence: "In him was life, and the life was the light of men." However, with the mention of light the transition is made from the realm of creation to the realm of history. Light can exist only in opposition to darkness; and thus a series of events are begun: "The light shines in the darkness, and the darkness has not overcome it." This is repeated, using other words, and in the second statement the Word of God is placed in the center of history:

> *He came to his own home,*
> *and his own people received him not.*
> *But to all who received him, . . .*
> *he gave power to become children of God.*

> (John 1:11-12)

Along with the statement, "He came to his own," we must hear the words, "*it* came," although this statement already has the ring of "he" from the sentence which follows: "The Word became flesh."

In this three-part sentence from the prologue we have a description of the focal point of all history. It contains all the history reported in both the Old and New Testaments. The Word of God always has produced an event which could be described in these three stages, whether it be in the Old or New Testament, or even in the history of his Word up to our present day.

Wherever a word of God went forth to a group of people—whether at the time of the wandering in the wilderness, during the Israelite monarchy, during the ministry of Jesus, in the period of the Reformation, or in a church of our present day—it found only the partial acceptance which has marked its entire history. Nevertheless, the Word always finds a few, a little band or a single individual, who accept it, and through these few there arises a history of the children of God.

In the sentence with which the prologue closes it is stated that this history belongs with the Word of God. The fact that God in his Word involves the realm of history implies that there is no Word of God apart from history.

This is further illustrated by the general structure of the Gospel of John. The three parts of this statement reappear as the three parts in the general structure of the Gospel. "He came to his own" is related in the first six chapters as they unfold what this coming means. "And his own people received him not" corresponds to the predominant characteristic in Chapters 7 through 12 where each act and each word of Jesus is met with opposition which becomes more and more intense until, at the end of Chapter 12, it points ahead to his rejection and final sentencing to death. "But to all who received him . . . he gave power to become children of God," is a description of the contents of Chapters 13 through 17 where Jesus talks with his disciples and prepares them for what is to come. However, all three parts come together in the conclusion to the Gospel, the report of the passion and resurrection of Jesus which John shares with the three Synoptic Gospels.

Therefore the evangelist's purpose in designing this magnificently clear and simple structure for his Gospel cannot be questioned. He wanted to report the history of God's Word in our world as it finally and conclusively ran its course in the life, passion, and resurrection of the man Jesus of Nazareth. John could do this only because he reckoned himself among those to whom this final Word of God went forth, because he placed himself in the line of witnesses to this history and joined in the confession of the community of believers:

We beheld his glory . . . .
(John 1:14)

The same thing was intended at the close of the first part of his Gospel when John reported that many were turning their backs upon Jesus. Peter answered Jesus' question concerning whether the disciples also wished to go away by saying, "You have the words of eternal life" (John 6:68).

What the Bible means by Word of God could not have been portrayed more beautifully and forcibly than it is here portrayed in John's Gospel. Here the relationship of God's Word to the far-reaching horizons of creation and history is clarified. It also becomes clear that a word of God, where it touches our human sphere, must become involved in history and must give rise to an event: The Word goes forth, it encounters rejection, it is nevertheless accepted by a few, and these few begin the way of faith. This applies to Jesus himself and to the words he spoke. It also applies to the words God spoke in many and various ways to the fathers of old. Thus we experience the Word of God only in connection with this occurrence, never apart from it.

For this reason the Bible is not a textbook, nor is it a collection of words of God; it is a history of the going forth of God's Word. A basic misunderstanding is revealed when the Bible is approached as a collection of timelessly valid statements from which one can extract any arbitrary statement, remove it from its context, and designate it as God's Word. This is already reflected in the external structure of the Old Testament; the first part contains a historical report; the second part contains the Word of God as it went forth to Israel through the prophets, and the third part contains the response to the Word in the prayers and hymns of those for whom the Word had been intended. Studying the Word of God and the words of God within the context of the entire Bible will enable us to hear it anew in each new age, for the historical nature of God's Word signifies at the same time its inexhaustibility.

Chapter XIII

The Law

According to the tables of contents in many of our Bibles, both the Old and New Testaments begin with a section entitled "historical books." However, the titles of the historical books in each Testament do not seem to have anything in common. Instead, these titles point out one of the major antitheses in the Bible. The first books in the New Testament are Gospels; the first books in the Old Testament are the Law or, in Hebrew, the *Torah*. Here we have a concept which is much more controversial than most other biblical concepts, yet a concept which is of vital significance in understanding the Bible. This concept of "law" played a decisive role in the separation of the Christian community from the Jewish community and, again, in the separation of the Reformation Church from the Roman Catholic Church.

Our understanding of the word "law" has been decisively influenced from two sharply differing realms: from the political realm through the concept of law as the regulation of a political structure, and from the realm of natural science through the concept of natural law. In both instances the use of the term is associated with the character of the absolute and necessary; the entire realm stands or falls depending upon the absolute validity of the law which is current in it. In this way we understand law and legality only within a limited realm, and the terms can vary greatly in the different realms in which we encounter them. Today we can scarcely comprehend what political laws could have in common with natural laws. The former are established by man; the latter are for man to discover, and man has nothing to do with their establishment or stability.

It is from this point that we can illustrate what the Bible means by law. The Bible presupposes that the entire world is God's domain, that nature and history are simply different provinces of God's sovereignty, and that all things therefore are governed by the same order. Thus, when the Bible speaks of law it is referring to that which orders and guides this entire domain.

The Book of Job contains a passage which somewhat enlightens this concept of law:

> *"Or who shut in the sea with doors, when it burst forth . . .*
> *when I . . . prescribed bounds for it, and set bars and doors,*
> *and said, 'Thus far shall you come, and no farther,*
> *and here shall your proud waves be stayed'?"*
>
> (Job 38:8-11)

Here we have in poetic language a description of what we call natural law. It is described in such a way, however, that we can detect a historical process, the stipulating command of One who possesses great power. It is to this comprehensive unity that the Bible refers when it speaks of God's law. Law is that order which embraces all things and determines all things; it is directly ordained by God and directly expresses his will for the entire world.

What was originally understood as law is affirmed throughout the entire Bible. For this reason we encounter statements by Paul in which he fully affirms the Law, even in his sharpest polemic against it. The statement in the Sermon on the Mount that not one letter of the Law shall pass away (Matt. 5:18) refers again to this total sovereignty of God over all realms of existence.

At first this sovereignty could not be expressed in any other manner than in the act of commanding, as we heard it in the command to the rebellious sea in the Book of Job. The creation also is presented as a series of commands: "For he spoke, and it came to be; he commanded, and it stood forth" (Psalm 33:9). The deliverance of Israel out of Egypt began with a command from God, and during the entire period of wandering in the wilderness the Israelites were led by commands and orders mediated through Moses. The story of Abraham begins with the command to depart from his homeland.

The situation is no different in the New Testament, as is expressed above all in Jesus' command to discipleship when he called his disciples (Matt. 4:18 ff., 9:9, etc.). In all these instances, the activity of God was carried out through a command directed to a person or group of persons, and in each instance the command was a vehicle of God's saving activity.

Only in this way can we comprehend the fact that first the command and then the Law could be given such positive significance in the Old Testament, or that the Law could be brought into such an intimate and insoluble relationship to history. Thus the Law is always viewed as a direct expression of God's goodness. As von Rad says in his *Old Testament Theology I:* "And right down to the end Israel sang its praises of the revelation of the divine will for justice as a saving blessing of a very high order." [1] And in the 119th Psalm, which is a very late psalm, when the worshiper can say:

> *If thy law had not been my comfort,*[2]
> *I should have perished in my affliction.*
> (Psalm 119:92)

then it becomes clear that the Law was for him a direct expression of the saving will of God.

How, then, could it occur that in the New Testament, first Jesus and then Paul had to come out in harsh opposition to the Law, indeed that it could reach the point where the total message of Christ was presented as opposing the Law? The answer to this question can be found in the history of the Law throughout the Old Testament.

This is a moving, violent history. Let us view it from the end. When Jesus was asked the question, "What must I do to inherit eternal life?" (Mark 10:17), and when he was asked to point out the greatest commandment (Matt. 22:36), the concern of the questioner was not for religious precepts, proper ethics, or a religious moral law; he was concerned about the order which regulates the stability of the world as a whole. This order had become controversial. When the question was raised, "What must I do?" it became

---

[1] Gerhard von Rad, *Old Testament Theology I: The Theology of Israel's Historical Traditions,* trans. by D. M. G. Stalker (New York: Harper & Row, 1962), p. 195.

[2] Translator's Note: Here the RSV reads, "had not been my delight."

apparent that adherence to the Law no longer was taken for granted. When someone asked about the greatest commandment, a distinction already was made between important and less important commandments. From these questions it is clear that the Old Testament law of God was not given to man in such a way that man could make it his own possession, like a piece of property. Rather, man received it only in the broken form of a historical phenomenon.

The clearest indication of this historical limitation to the Law is reflected in the enormous effort which, during the centuries before the birth of Christ, was directed toward the interpretation of the Law and its application to changing situations of the time. Had the Law been a timeless entity, always valid in every respect, its meaning and application would also have been clear in every new situation, without need of interpretation.

There is something truly tragic about this striving after the Law in late Judaism. The Law contained an abundance of commands, statutes, and ordinances intended for a period in the life of the people which long since had passed. There were commands for conducting wars, but the Jewish province no longer had any wars to conduct. There were regulations concerning kingship and prophecy, but these also no longer existed. On the other hand, there arose questions for which the Law had no answer, as illustrated by this question once directed to Jesus: "Is it lawful to pay taxes to Caesar?" (Matt. 22:17)

In spite of these obvious historical limitations of the Law, the Jewish community adhered to it as the revealed will of God with a passion and vigor which no longer is explicable. It would be too superficial and of little value to see here only the easily criticized casuistry, such as the splitting of hairs over all those things that one dare not do on the Sabbath. Furthermore, we should never overlook the fact that to take with such seriousness the revelation of the will of God, which had spanned centuries and had determined the entire history of a people, should in itself demand recognition and respect, even in this exaggerated form.

Only in this light does it become clear what Jesus meant in his criticism of the Law. For one must speak in terms of criticism when Jesus could say something like this: "The sabbath was made for man, not man for the sabbath . . . " (Mark 2:27), or " . . . not what goes into the mouth defiles a man, but what comes out of the mouth, this defiles a man" (Matt. 15:11). Over the centuries the Jewish community had come to view the Law more and more as a prescribed entity which was completely at its disposal. One could say, "We have the Law." Here Jesus appeared in defense of the spontaneity of God's will. The Law as an expression of God's will was no less holy to Jesus than it was to the Jewish scribes, but he could secure due recognition for this will of God only by pointing from the limitation of the written Law to the living will of God.

Here is a tragic irony: In his criticism Jesus simply pointed back to the beginning of the Law, exposing its original meaning. When someone asked him about the way to eternal life and Jesus referred him to the Ten Commandments (Matt. 19:16 ff.), this was in accord with his criticism of the Law. By this Jesus did not want to imply, however, that the Ten Commandments formed the good and proper core of the Law and everything else that had been added was evil. Neither should this imply that he affirmed the ethical law but rejected the cultic law.

The solution is to be found more along these lines: A command can be an expression of the living will of God in a way essentially different from that of a law. We have become accustomed to speaking of command and law in the same breath, as though a law consisted of individual commands. Research into this whole complex of laws has revealed that there is a substantial difference between command and law. A command originates from a personal address: "You shall not kill" (Ex. 20:14). A law has the characteristics of a statute: "Whoever strikes a man so that he dies shall be put to death" (Ex. 21:12). These two basic forms, command and law, have different origins, and only in the course of a long history were they so bound together that law became the over-all concept for individual commands. Thus, as the command became overshadowed by the Law, a development was introduced which eventually transformed the Law into an independent entity which Jesus no longer could acknowledge as a genuine expression of the will of God.

This process can be seen already in a section of Old Testament literature which stems from an early period. The revelation of the Law at Mount Sinai originally was presented in varying accounts, which later were joined together to form one continuous narrative.

However, here the various voices from the different periods can still be recognized. In the earlier account, the commandments were given orally by God (Ex. 20:1-17), even as Moses transmitted them orally to the people (Ex. 24:3). Later it was expressly added that Moses recorded all the commandments (Ex. 24:4). Still later the original written form of the Law was further strengthened when it was asserted that God himself wrote "the law and the commandment" on the tablets and then handed them over to Moses (Ex. 24:12). For each of these three stages in the tradition there are other parallels. For instance, at the end of the first major section of the Priestly Code it is stated with emphasis that "he gave to Moses . . . the two tables of the testimony, tables of stone, written with the finger of God" (Ex. 31:18).

The purpose of this later account was not to report an especially striking miracle (as it was portrayed, for example, in the movie "The Ten Commandments"). The sole concern of this account was to insure the written form of the Law beyond a shadow of a doubt by tracing it directly back to God. The compilers of these stories who allowed the older account, in which the proclamation and transmission of the commandments took place orally, to remain beside this account thus made it obvious that they did not consider the writing of the Law by the finger of God as the only authentic account of what happened.

When seen from the point of view of history, the two accounts of the giving of the Law reflect two stages in the tradition of the Law: the earlier tradition in which the commandments of God are proclaimed and transmitted orally, and the later tradition in which the Law acquired its written form and in which the written tradition is predominant. With these two points we have indicated the path from the command of God to the Law of God. At that point where the Law takes the place of the command we have the beginning of the autonomy and then the hardening of the Law. This whole process has just been uncovered for us by recent research.

Chapter XIV

Formation of the Law

The distinction between command and law in the Old Testament puts the significance of the Ten Commandments, the only segment of Old Testament Law to be adopted without reservation by the Christian church, into a new light. After scholars had long assumed that the Ten Commandments originated during a relatively late period, it now is overwhelmingly agreed that they belong to the earliest period in Israel's history even if they did undergo changes later.

In addition to the Ten Commandments, there are various other short series of commandments in which the commands or prohibitions all have a similar form. This observation first received major attention in a study by Albrecht Alt which had a revolutionary effect.[1] Alt discovered that the so-called "Covenant Code" (Ex. 21–23) contained several such series of individual commands similar to those found in the Ten Commandments. Their common characteristic was their brief, apodictic (or absolute) form, and they could have been intended only for oral presentation and transmission. When one considers the fact that they all are in the form of direct address—"You shall not . . . "—it becomes almost self-evident that these series of commands once were spoken in public worship, where the speaker would speak in the name of God and where the listeners would consider themselves directly addressed by the Word of God.

---

[1] Albrecht Alt, "The Origins of Israelite Law," in *Essays on Old Testament and Religion*, trans. by R. S. Wilson (Garden City, N.Y.: Doubleday & Co., Inc., 1968), pp. 101-172. This study first appeared in German in 1934.

In addition to the apodictic laws, Alt found another, completely different form of law in the Covenant Code. According to this form, a judicial case would be presented and a judgment rendered, such as, "If a man borrows anything of his neighbor, and it is hurt or dies, the owner not being with it, he shall make full restitution" (Ex. 22:14). In a much earlier period in the ancient Near East— for example, from the time of the Code of Hammurabi—one finds amazing parallels to this casuistic (that is, conditional or case) law of the Covenant Code. These parallels correspond both in form and in content. On the other hand, in all these legal codes from the ancient Near East not one parallel has been found to the apodictic commands (such as those found in the Ten Commandments).

Alt came to the conclusion, which has won widespread acceptance, that the apodictic commands are examples of the oldest form of divine command used in Israel from the time of the wandering in the wilderness. When the Israelites entered the civilized land of Canaan, they adopted the legal forms current there to the extent that this seemed necessary for their new sedentary way of life, and to the extent that these new legal forms seemed compatible with Israel's own understanding of divine justice. Thus we have an indication of the theological significance of this remarkable uniting of sharply divergent forms of commands and laws in the Covenant Code: The people of Israel, even as they adopted many of the customs of their new land, also had the freedom to take part in the judicial structure of this new world.

Israel did not thereby do away with the old revelation of God's will; rather, she added the new laws to the old commands. If these now are combined in one body of law, it simply means that Israel also heard the new laws as the command of God given to her when she became a people: "I am the Lord your God. . . . You shall have no other gods besides me" (Ex. 20:2-3). And it means, further, that we now find added to the original command of God ordinances which were not so directly revealed by God and which were not so directly his word.

The history of the Law in Israel is not herewith closed. The Covenant Code is followed in later periods of Israel's history by other codes, such as the Deuteronomic Code contained in the Book of Deuteronomy; the Holiness Code; and the Priestly Code, which does not appear until the period after the Exile. All of these can still be recognized as complete and independent law codes extending in the above order of succession over the entire history of Israel. As is the case everywhere in the history of law, these laws become more inclusive as they move from one stage to the next. They increase in content from the short series of commands in the Decalogue to the three chapters of the Covenant Code, and finally to the Priestly Code, which includes everything from Exodus 25 through Numbers 10. The latter is the result of the efforts of several generations of priestly scholars. It contains several stages in the development of priestly legislation, as well as individual collections of priestly laws. Several of these codes still reflect the period from which they originated; in the Deuteronomic Code, for example, one can clearly detect the influence of prophecy.

This whole colorful complex of diverse laws, commands, statutes, and ordinances, formed in a centuries-long process of development, has become attached to a single point in Israel's history: the revelation of God at Mount Sinai. Viewed historically, this process remains far removed from us; we can no longer reconstruct it. However, one thing is clear from accounts of the early history of the people of Israel: The little band of Israelites became a people through the experience of a miracle of God, and the revelation of God's will stands in an inextricable relationship to that miracle at the beginning. There cannot be the one without the other. This is expressed in the concept of the covenant which God established with his people and which can be reduced to this simple formula: "I will be your God, and you shall be my people" (cf. Ex. 6:7, Jer. 30:22, 32:38, etc.). Old Testament law is anchored in this statement which informs Israel how she can be God's people. And Israel wants to be God's people, because he has dealt miraculously with her.

This is the essential reason all Old Testament laws were grouped around the revelation at Sinai. When the narratives of the Pentateuch present all these laws, from the Ten Commandments to the comprehensive Priestly Code, in such a way that they are reported to have been revealed by God at Mount Sinai through Moses, this is not intended to be a historical account in our sense of the term. Those who compiled the later collections of law were fully aware of the historical gap between the earlier and the later laws. They made no attempt to smooth over the evidence of additions to the laws, or the differences and even contradictions between earlier and later laws, or the many insertions and later corrections. They did nothing to destroy or even diminish the impression that these laws originated gradually through a process which covered centuries.

However, it is understandable that this awareness of the gradual formation of the law eventually would fade, and this great complex of laws would come to be understood as an independent entity, as *the* Law. At this point the formerly predominant commands also were made subordinate to the Law and became part of it. Here we can also detect another basic shift: The Law became the most important factor in the pentateuchal account of Israel's early history, dominating the entire account. For this reason this historical narrative was given the name "Torah," that is, "Law."

But in spite of this development, we must recognize that the heart of the Pentateuch is still basically a historical acccount which grew out of the confession and praise of the great acts of God. Thus, when the Law became the predominant factor in the pentateuchal narrative, a fundamental change took place in the meaning of the Pentateuch. The change led to making the Law absolute, which Jesus so strongly opposed.

At this point we can illustrate how modern biblical research, which is often viewed with great suspicion, has once again brought to light a fundamental biblical fact. At the close of the last century, Julius Wellhausen, the German theologian, and his followers brought about a revolutionary change in the understanding of the formation of the Pentateuch which had held sway up until that time. It had been assumed that the level of tradition containing the laws was the oldest level of tradition in the Pentateuch. Wellhausen demonstrated that the tradition containing the Priestly Code, the latest level of tradition, did not originate until after the time of the prophets, perhaps during the Exile or even later.[2] This meant that the Priestly Code, rather than standing at the beginning of Israel's history, now stood close to the end. It did not belong to the revelation at Sinai, but was transferred there at a later time.

Wellhausen's hypothesis became established, even if it did have to undergo some major corrections. However, this hypothesis ob-

---

[2] Cf. esp. *op. cit.*, *Prologomena to the History of Israel.*

scured the fact that the Priestly Code did not comprise the Law per se, but that it, too, had a complicated prehistory which spanned centuries. Since Wellhausen, much research has been done on this prehistory. Albrecht Alt,[3] for example, discovered that the apodictic commands such as the Ten Commandments, elements of which are also found in the Priestly Code (Ex. 34), belong to the earliest period of Israel's history. Thus, even though the Priestly Code as a collection of laws is of relatively late origin, it contains laws which stem from a very early period. This confirms what the Old Testament is saying when it designates the Ten Commandments as the regulations for the covenant which God established with his people at the beginning of their history.

We have been able to present the history of Old Testament law only in roughest outline. We must add that the term "Torah," in the sense of "law," is a later, general concept which absorbed within itself the more specific vocabulary of command, regulation, and statute. Originally "Torah" meant instruction which had come from God. What is essential is the fact that we no longer can view the Law as a single, all-inclusive law given to the people of Israel at Mount Sinai. Instead, by recognizing the fact that the Old Testament contains a whole series of law codes which originated one after the other over the course of Israel's history, we have reached an almost unanimously accepted basis for further research on the Law. This conclusion has been accepted not only by Protestant and Roman Catholic scholars but by Jewish scholars as well, a fact which is of great significance for further discussion of Old Testament law.

To understand the relationship between the Old and New Testaments, it is important to recognize that Paul still understood the Law as a closed entity, a view which we no longer accept today. Whenever Paul places faith in Christ in opposition to the works of the Law, he is referring to the Law as a way of salvation, a means by which one becomes justified before God through one's own deeds. This concept of law, however, cannot do justice to the history of command and law in the Old Testament.

---

[3] *Op. cit.,* "The Origins of Israelite Law."

Chapter XV

The Sermon on the Mount

Toward the beginning of the Sermon on the Mount we find that Jesus rather abruptly set his own commands against several commands from the Decalogue: "You have heard that it was said to the men of old, 'You shall not kill . . . . ' But I say to you that every one who is angry with his brother shall be liable to judgment" (Matt. 5:21-22). Here Jesus intensifies the old commands to such an extent that the question concerning the purpose of these intense, radical demands and also the purpose of the Sermon on the Mount itself has never been silenced. Up to the present time the Sermon on the Mount has been a center of controversy, even in the church. For example, to this day one cannot point to a single instance where the church has clearly outlined the practical implications of the command to abstain from resisting evil in terms of the abruptness and finality with which Jesus presents it here.

It is therefore understandable that most explanations of the Sermon on the Mount have attempted to limit the validity of its demands. In an essay in his book on the life of Jesus, Günther Bornkamm speaks of a "fatal only" which shines through all explanations of the sermon.[1] It had been assumed that Jesus had intended these sayings in the Sermon on the Mount only for the interim period before his return. Thus, the demands were to be understood merely as exceptions in time of crisis, each serving as a last rousing call to obedience in the face of the fast-approaching

---

[1] *Op. cit.,* Appendix II, "The History of the Exposition of the Sermon on the Mount," pp. 221-25.

Day of Judgment. This view that the Sermon on the Mount contains an interim ethic was represented especially by Johannes Weiss and Albert Schweitzer.[2]

An opposite approach is taken by those who see in Jesus' radical demands an impossible ideal and consider this to be their essential purpose. The Sermon on the Mount, so they say, attempts to make man aware of his inability to satisfy God's higher demands, and thus in the face of such impossible demands it moves man to rely solely on God's forgiving grace. According to this interpretation, the sermon has the same task which Paul ascribes to the Law: to lead us to an awareness of our sins because it can never be fulfilled in its entirety. But here it becomes obvious that the Sermon on the Mount is being interpreted through the eyes of Paul. In the sermon itself there is no indication that the above is intended.

A third common interpretation attempts to extract from the sermon a principle which could be used to set up a political or social system or program. This approach can be seen in Tolstoy's *Resurrection*.[3] In my opinion, this reflects an encounter with the Sermon which is more real and earnest than the principles that Tolstoy then, in his experiments and theoretical writings, deduced from it. All attempts at making the lofty demands of Jesus serve a political or social program were simply not in accord with the reality of the situation during this period. The demands of the Sermon on the Mount cannot be incorporated into a social or political system because they obviously were not intended for that purpose.

We will come closer to understanding the Sermon on the Mount if we remember that the simple commands from Israel's early history were eventually united with her laws and that this body of laws grew larger and larger in direct correspondence to the increase in her population and the extension of her national boundaries. However, the will of God as expressed in these few early commands receded into the background behind the comprehensive Law over which the people now held control, and through which they felt they had direct access to the will of God.

---

[2] Cf. esp. Johannes Weiss, *Die Predigt Jesu vom Reich Gottes,* second ed. (Göttingen: Vanderhoeck and Ruprecht, 1964). First German edition, 1892. Albert Schweitzer, *The Mystery of the Kingdom of God* (London: A. & C. Black, 1956). First German edition 1901. Cf. also, Schweitzer, *op. cit.*

[3] Leo Tolstoy, *Resurrection* (London: Oxford University Press, 1928). First published in 1900.

The message of Jesus broke through this wall which the Law had erected and paved the way for a return to the clarity and directness of the simple command of God. Thus, whenever he was approached with a question, Jesus could simply refer the questioner to these commands. There are other instances in which Jesus reaffirmed the validity of the ancient command of God. For example, when the Sabbath commandment had been perverted by the influence of the Law, he brought out its original purpose—to preserve God's gift of a day for rest. It is therefore out of the question to assume that Jesus wished to declare the Ten Commandments invalid and to replace those commands with the radical demands of the Sermon on the Mount. The church acted wisely when, in spite of the antitheses of the Sermon on the Mount, she incorporated the Ten Commandments into her teaching. The Ten Commandments are not abolished or superseded in the Gospels: they are once again given their due respect as commands of God.

Thus something fundamentally different from the Law, or even the commands, must have been intended by Jesus in the Sermon on the Mount. The Sermon on the Mount was not a new law, but it also was not a new series of commandments. And our modern concepts are equally inadequate. Joachim Jeremias is correct when he says, "In order to make the difference clear, one should avoid . . . the terms 'Christian ethic,' 'Christian morality,' 'Christian morals,' because these secular expressions are inadequate and liable to misunderstanding. Instead of these, one should speak of 'lived faith' *(gelebter Glaube)*." [4] He also writes, "what is here taught is symptoms, signs, examples, of what it means when the Kingdom of God breaks into the world which is still under sin, death, and the devil." [5] Another interpreter calls the Sermon on the Mount the proclamation of the entrance requirements for the coming rule of God. [6]

What is essential here, however, is the fact that the sayings in the Sermon on the Mount point to a new potential in human behavior which has been opened up through the dawning of a new

---

[4] Joachim Jeremias, *The Sermon on the Mount,* trans. Norman Perrin (Philadelphia: Fortress Press, A Facet Book, 1963), p. 34.
[5] *Ibid.,* p. 33.
[6] H. Windisch, *The Meaning of the Sermon on the Mount,* trans. S. MacLean Gilmour (Philadelphia: Westminster Press, 1951), pp. 27 ff., 36 f., 199 f.

age in man's relationship to God. Every saying also points to the fact that, with the coming of Christ, something has taken place which will transform this world to its very foundations. However, since the kingly rule of God is still hidden, the demands of a radically changed mode of human behavior also cannot be considered law or command in the traditional sense. They are rather signs which point to the dawning of a new reality.

What this signifies becomes clearer once we understand how the Sermon on the Mount was formed. Anyone who carefully reads it will understand that this was not a sermon in our present sense of the term. These chapters of Matthew 5 through 7 are a collection of individual sayings. This can be seen without any special knowledge or training. Matthew put these sayings together in a simple manner to form a continuous address, through the use of the introductory sentences of Chapter 5:1-2 and the closing sentence in Chapter 7:28. A similar but shorter compilation is formed by the Sermon on the Plain in Luke 6:20-49. The similarity between the two—both begin with the Beatitudes—indicates that both evangelists had access to a shorter compilation which each expanded in his own way and incorporated into his own Gospel.

In the case of Matthew, a definite structure is discernible. The collection of Jesus' sayings in Chapters 5 through 7 is followed by a collection of miracle stories in Chapters 8 and 9. Matthew thereby unfolds in his Gospel a confessional statement which says concerning Jesus that he was "mighty in deed and word" (cf. Luke 24:19, Acts 2:22).

This observation can result in an important conclusion for our understanding of the Sermon on the Mount: If the sayings of the sermon were first collected by Matthew and then put into the framework of an address by Jesus, and if each of the sayings once circulated independently, then we must first listen to each of these sayings as an independent saying if we want to understand its original meaning. At the same time we must be aware of the fact that we do not know the context in which Jesus originally spoke these sayings. Let us pause for a moment and listen to one especially difficult saying in Chapter 5:

> *"If your right eye causes you to sin, pluck it out and throw it away"* (Matt. 5:29).

This statement follows the saying concerning divorce, so that in this context it could be referring only to the eye which looks lustfully at another man's wife. However, we do not know if this is the original context of the saying. It is much more feasible that Jesus said this in a completely different context, which we no longer know today—for example, within the context of discipleship.

On the other hand, in the story of the rich young man and his question about how to attain eternal life, Jesus told him to sell all that he had and give the proceeds to the poor (Matt. 19:16-22). Here one of Jesus' radical demands is transmitted within the context of a definite situation. Were we to detach the demand from this particular situation, its meaning would be fundamentally changed; it does not have the character of a law or a command. It was an extraordinary demand, happening only once and having its meaning only in relationship to this particular man in this specific moment.

We must think along the same lines concerning the statements on plucking out an eye or turning the other cheek (Matt. 5:39). Each of these sayings was once spoken in a specific, solitary situation which we no longer know. None of these sayings attempted to be universally valid, like a command or law. Here again, each saying should be a sign pointing to a new potentiality which has been opened up through the coming of Christ.

Thus it becomes clear what Matthew was attempting to say when he compiled such sayings into the Sermon on the Mount. He was not compiling a set of Christian rules for living; rather, he was attempting to direct our attention to that point where a breakthrough is reflected in these sayings. This accounts for the essentially impossible concentration of so many abrupt demands. In this density they form a hymn of triumph, the mighty word of Jesus which opens up the potentiality for human behavior beyond our subjection to the almighty "I," with all its needs and demands. They become a challenge to our world of mediocrity and restraint.

When understood in this light, the Sermon on the Mount demands constant alertness. Everyone who reads it must be aware of the questions which are directed at him, asking whether the sign of such action is being expected of him, in his situation, whether *one* of the sayings of the sermon could be addressed specifically to him, precisely in that moment when he hears the saying. It is entirely in accord with the meaning of the sermon that persons outside the Christian community would again hear a saying from the sermon after it had long been silenced, would take that saying seriously, and by acting in accordance with it would raise up a sign which once again would direct many to the living Christ.

I would like to close this chapter with a word from an essay by Günther Bornkamm:

> In following this history we find ourselves faced with the question whether the times when the Sermon on the Mount has had special historical significance were not always those in which men allowed themselves to be challenged by Jesus' demand and commandment in a radical and direct fashion, and sought, with the most thoroughgoing personal decision, to put the Sermon on the Mount into practice, quite literally in their own day—in their refusal to take an oath, by their renunciation of personal property, their "no" to military service. Were not these the truly historical moments, in which the crumbling foundations of the supposedly sacred political, social, moral and religious traditions were shaken, where the volcano of the Sermon on the Mount erupted, or at least where its menacing glow of fire became visible, whose light revealed the precarious ledge upon which Christianity had settled down to a comfortable existence, and upon which unconcernedly it let the flocks of the faithful graze? [7]

---

[7] *Op. cit.*, Appendix II, "The History of the Exposition of the Sermon on the Mount," p. 221.

Chapter XVI

The Secret of the Parables

One of Jesus' parables ends with the statement: "He who has ears to hear, let him hear" (Matt. 11:15, etc.). In other words, anyone who really listens can understand the parables; beyond this there are no other prerequisites.

The Old Testament tells the story of Nathan, the prophet, who appeared before King David after the king had committed a grave wrong (2 Sam. 12). Nathan told David how a rich man had taken a poor man's only lamb and had used it to feed a guest, even though the rich man possessed many flocks. This story had nothing to do with David's own sin, yet he became intensely involved when he himself was made judge of the case. He became enraged and demanded a stiff sentence for the rich man. At this point Nathan said to him: "You are the man!" Here it is evident that understanding the parable involves seeing a relationship between what the parable relates and the one to whom the parable refers.

However, the parables in the Gospels seem to be an entirely different matter. How much has been read into these parables! How the understanding of them has changed over the course of time, and what uncertainty reigns in the exposition of the parables to this very day! What is the reason for all this? This much has been answered for us today after extensive research. The reason lies in the fact that, in the case of most of Jesus' parables, we no longer know the exact situation in which they originally were given. Nathan's

parable is clear because it has been transmitted to us together with
the exact situation to which it originally was directed. Imagine, for
a moment, that we had received Nathan's parable without knowing
to whom or in what situation it had been presented. How many
possibilities for interpretation would arise!

We could further add that Nathan's parable illustrates the fact
that in every parable two different incidents are placed side by
side. The meaning of a parable can be understood only when one
reflects upon the occurrence related in the parable, an occurrence
which is complete in itself, and then places this beside the occurrence which the parable is to clarify, an occurrence equally complete in itself. In Nathan's parable this is self-evident. But it becomes more difficult if one knows only the parable and nothing
about the person or the situation to which it was addressed. Here
two courses could be followed in interpreting the parables. One
could attempt to interpret each feature of the parable independently,
as having reference to a different, hidden meaning. This would
transform the parable into an allegory, and would transfer the meaning of the parable to a timeless plain. Or one could attempt to deduce from the parable a general teaching, whereby one no longer
would need to know the specific situation for which the parable
was originally coined.

Both of these alternatives are often encountered in the parables
of Jesus as they have been transmitted to us in the Gospels. The
first alternative is seen, for example, in the parable of the sower
and the seed, where an interpretation has been added giving an
explanation of each feature of the parable (Mark 4:3-9, the parable,
Mark 4:14-20, the interpretation). The same is true of the parable
concerning the tares among the wheat (Matt. 13:36-43). In both
instances the language reveals that the interpretation originated
among the followers of Jesus. But here, as at other points in the
Gospels, we have only the earliest beginnings of allegorical interpretation. It was not until later that this method of interpretation
came into full blossom as we know it from the early Christian and
medieval periods.

The other alternative—the attempt to deduce a general teaching
from the parable—is illustrated by the concluding sentences in many
of the parables. For example, when the same concluding statement, "For many are called, but few are chosen," stands at the close

of two entirely different parables (the parable of the workers in the vineyard in Matthew 20:1-16 [1] and the parable of the marriage feast in Matthew 22:1-14); or when the same parable, recorded in two different Gospels, ends with a different closing statement; or when one account of a parable has two different closing statements (Matt. 20:16),[2] one can conclude that this closing statement is the result of a later interpretation of the parable.

Both of these possibilities for later modification of the parables by means of an added interpretation are encountered with such frequency in the Gospels that we are led to a conclusion which is very important for both the history and the understanding of the parables. In many of the parables we can distinguish two stages of development. The first stage contains the original account in which the parable received its meaning from the situation to which it was addressed. In this original setting, the parables were often directed at an opponent, at someone who was quite indifferent, or, at any rate, at an outsider. As the details of these original situations were lost and the parables were passed on without them, the question was raised concerning the meaning of the parables for the Christian community. Thus the transmission of the parables entered a second stage; now they were understood as directed at the followers of Jesus. In this process the meaning of the parables changed somewhat. It was during this second stage that the allegorical and general interpretations were added, almost all of which originated in the early Christian community.

This two-stage development of the parables indicates that the essential contents must be traced back to the proclamations of Jesus. Joachim Jeremias writes: "The parables are a fragment of the original rock of tradition." [3] From the present evidence one can conclude that the earlier stage of development is a necessary prerequisite to the parables as we now have them in the Gospels. To be sure, this makes the interpretation of the parables more difficult in many instances. We must assume that their original meaning often

---

[1] Translator's Note: Many ancient manuscripts include this statement as part of Matthew 20:16, but since the evidence from other reliable sources indicates that it is a later interpolation, it is not included in the text of the RSV.

[2] Cf. preceding Translator's Note.

[3] Joachim Jeremias, *The Parables of Jesus,* third edition (New York: Charles Scribner's Sons, 1955), p. 9.

does not correspond exactly to the meaning given to them in the early Christian community. And we must reckon with the fact that in many of the parables we may be able to surmise the original meaning but not be able to establish it with certainty.

Could this represent a great gain in our understanding of the parables and our heeding of their message? Does this mean that we will be able to understand these parables, which are so often all too hastily and assuredly explained, only when we proceed more carefully with our interpretations? Could the parables, then, have things to say which are not clearly heard in our present interpretations? Recognition that the parables have been transmitted to us with a later, partially modified interpretation could lead to renewed understanding of these parables and of the early Christian community and its problems.

Yet, we also encounter in the Gospels parables which show no signs of later attempts at interpretation. An example of this is found in the parable of the seed which grew by itself, presented here in a new translation by Günther Bornkamm:

> *The Kingdom of God is as*
> *if a man should scatter seed upon the ground,*
> *and should sleep and rise night and day,*
> *and the seed should sprout and grow up,*
> *he knows not how.*
> *The earth produces of itself,*
> *first the blade, then the ear, then the full grain in the ear.*
> *But when the grain is ripe,*
> *at once he (the master of the field) puts in the sickle, because*
> *the harvest has come.*[4]
>
> (Mark 4:26-29)

We can assume that this parable was first given by Jesus in answer to a question that had been directed to him or an attack that had been leveled against him. Bornkamm sees in it "an answer to a passionate striving of those who want to force the coming of the Kingdom of God."[5] It also could be the reply to a reproach which had dismissed Jesus' "hidden" activity as meaningless. What is important is the fact that no attempt was made to replace the unknown circumstances and locale of the parable through a later

---

[4] *Op. cit.*, p. 73. The English translation of Bornkamm's book follows the RSV which is almost exactly the same.
[5] *Ibid.*, p. 73.

interpretation. Thus the parable remained intact and direct. It compels us to simply listen again and again to what is related here. What it was intended to say then and what it can say today are clear from the story itself, without need of special explanation. The parable quite obviously centers around the statement, "The earth produces of itself."

However, "of itself" can be applied to the rule of God and its coming in a variety of ways, and here is where our questions concerning the interpretation set in. The same is true with many other parables. It is the nature of parables that questions related to them should remain open questions. The parable of the seed which grew by itself can never be interpreted conclusively for all time. It exists in the Gospels as a parable so that it can be spoken anew on each occasion when its message needs to be heard. Here we recognize the fact that a simple parable such as this is again and again brought forth to new life in the proclamation of the church.

The secret of the parables rests in their simplicity. One group has been called the contrast parables. An example is the double parable of the mustard seed and the leaven (Matt. 13:31-33, Luke 13:18-21). However, one could also call all the kingdom parables contrast parables, for they are all determined by the contrast between that which they allude to—the coming of the kingdom of God—and that of which they speak—an aspect of everyday life. For us it is an astonishing fact that a parable such as that of the seed which grew by itself (Mark 4:26-29), or of the mustard seed and the leaven (Matt. 13:31-32) should be able to speak entirely of itself, without a trace of interpretation, without a sign of theological language, but simply by presenting one small and inconspicuous aspect of the normal reality of our existence. Here the proclamation of Jesus stands in sharp contrast to all apocalyptic literature, which must erect the apparatus of a great mythological drama whenever it attempts to portray the coming of the kingdom.[6] In the parables con-

---

[6] Translator's Note: Here the author is referring to a type of literature which was common during the exilic and post-exilic periods and during some periods of early Christianity. It emphasized the opposing cosmic forces (the force of light or good, usually associated with God, and the force of darkness or evil) which at the end of this "evil" age were to engage in a dramatic cosmic battle, with the forces of God winning out and ushering in his eternal kingdom. Cf. also the author's reference to this type of literature on page 59 f.

cerning the kingdom, the incarnation of the Word of God is most clearly expressed. Here God has so entered the realm of our human existence that the beginning of his reign can be spoken of in a decidedly human manner, without any sign of the sacred or cultic.

The coming of God's reign can have two effects upon those to whom it comes: salvation or judgment. Accordingly, two distinct groups can be observed in the parables. Jeremias describes the purpose of the first group thus: "to shock into realization of its danger a nation rushing upon its own destruction, and more especially its leaders, the theologians and priests." [7]

To this group belong the parables dealing with the barren fig tree which was to be cut down if it did not bear fruit (Luke 13:6-9), the guest without a wedding garment (Matt. 22:11-14), the unforgiving servant (Matt. 18:23-35), the unjust steward (Luke 16:1-8), and the wise and foolish maidens (Matt. 25:1-13). Here Jesus took up the prophets' proclamation of doom and carried it to the end. Like the prophets, he placed special emphasis on the leadership, on those in positions of responsibility, as in the parable of the wicked tenants (Matt. 21:33-44, etc.), of the servant who was given authority (Matt. 24:45-51, Luke 12:42-46), and of the talents and the pounds (Matt. 25:14-30, Luke 19:12-27).

A second group of parables proclaims the coming salvation, but they do not deal with the age of salvation as such. We find, instead, a direct word which imparts salvation, as in the Beatitudes (Matt. 5:3-12); or an invitation to salvation, as in the Savior's own words, "Come to me, all who labor and are heavy-laden . . . " (Matt. 11:28). Instead of attempting to portray some future age of salvation, these parables are directed at Jesus' opponents in reply to their annoyance over his message of good news to the poor and lost. This is evident in the parable of the laborers in the vineyard, which closes with the question, "Do you begrudge my generosity?" (Matt. 20:15). Here belong also the three parables in Luke 15 dealing with those who are lost, the parable of the two debtors in Luke 7:41-43, the parable of the Pharisee and the publican in Luke 18:9-14, and many other similar parables. In all of these, Jesus is proclaiming the love of God which he himself is bringing to mankind, a love which is unlimited.

---

[7] *Op. cit.*, p. 126, *The Parables of Jesus.*

Because this sovereign rule of God was ushered in through the activity of a man among men, in sharp contrast to that which one otherwise associates with the assumption of rulership or the seizure of power, Jesus spoke in the form of parables. What, then, really is meant by the sovereign rule of God? This will be the subject of our next inquiry.

Chapter XVII

The Kings of Israel and the Kingly Rule of God

"The kingdom of heaven is like . . . "—so begin many of the parables in Luther's familiar translation of the Bible.[1] The mental imagery which we associate with the term "heaven" is almost of necessity incorrect, insofar as it usually is descriptive of a realm beyond our world. Whenever the phrase "kingdom of heaven" appears (which is only in the Gospel of Matthew) we should instead hear the phrase "kingdom of God," for in the language presumed to be behind the Gospel of Matthew "heaven" was a paraphrasis for "God," or could be used as such.[2] The other part of the phrase,

---

[1] Translator's Note: The author is here referring to the German version of the Bible as translated by Dr. Martin Luther. In terms of its widespread use even today, after more recent translations have appeared, and in terms of its impact upon the formation and preservation of the German language, this translation would correspond roughly to the King James version of the Bible among English-speaking people.

[2] Translator's Note: Here the author is not just referring to the Aramaic language, but to the entire language world of first century Judaism (during which Aramaic was the primary language). Although it is now widely accepted that the Gospel of Matthew was written in Greek for a Greek-speaking community, it is also generally agreed that the language of the oral traditions behind the Gospel was definitely Aramaic and that the Gospel itself has a distinctly Jewish-Christian character, having originated as the result of a direct encounter between Christianity and Judaism. In late Judaism, as the author indicates, it was common to show reverence for God by avoiding the use of the divine name, and by substituting, instead, such synonymous phrases as "kingdom of God" or "kingdom of heaven." Thus the Jewish *Targum*, an extensive commentary on the Old Testament, in commenting on Isaiah 40:9, "Behold your God," substitutes "The kingdom of your God has become manifest."

"kingdom," does not refer so much to a specific domain over which God rules as it does to the exercise of that rule itself. A more precise translation of the Greek word *basileia* would be sovereignty, kingship, or kingly rule.

Unfortunately, this phrase has become so worn that we are scarcely able to hear its specific meaning. When viewed from our perspective, "kingly rule of God" is a contradiction because here a strictly political concept is used to describe the divine nature of God and the message of Christ, which truly has no political character whatsoever. How is this to be understood?

In the cultural milieu from which Israel originated, there existed centuries before Israel's appearance on the historical scene a phenomenon known as divine kingship in which the king stood in direct relationship to the deity. This relationship expressed itself in several forms. It could mean that the king was worshiped as a god, or that he was descended from the gods; it could mean that he had been adopted by a god, or that at his death he would become a god. Whatever the specific form of the relationship, the king always participated in the realm of the sacred; his nature was conceived as being somewhere between that of the gods and that of the people, thereby also bestowing upon him the function of intermediary. Thus throughout this entire area there existed some form of cult—an entire system of worship—which centered around the king and in which the king himself played an essential role. He might represent a god, or he might represent the people before the gods, in which case he would either mediate the divine blessing to his people or serve as intercessor for his people.

In all the cultures of the ancient Near East the king and the deity stood in closest relationship to each other. Often the gods were depicted as reigning kings, and it was common everywhere to speak of the government of the gods.

Kingship was introduced relatively late in Israel and, in contrast to the surrounding area, it never developed into a divine kingship, although there are traces of such a phenomenon in the Old Testament. In one isolated instance, found in Psalm 45, the king is referred to as God, and several of the royal psalms show evidence of the king's relationship to the sacred sphere. It appears that remnants of an old, pre-Israelite royal priesthood lived on, above all, in the Jerusalem tradition and were incorporated into the coronation rites of the Israelite kings. Evidence of this still can be recognized in the royal psalms (such as Psalms 18, 20, 21, 72). On the whole, however, one factor which set Israel apart was the fact that Israel did not regard her kings as divine. For this reason, the history of kingship in Israel was marked by deep tensions right from the beginning.

Kingship was introduced in Israel at the time the Israelite tribes, now settled in Canaan, were so hard-pressed by the Philistines that a central political authority became necessary. This is reported in the First Book of Samuel where we can see that there also existed a group which passionately rejected the introduction of kingship. This group argued that a mere human being could not be king, and to bestow upon a man the rank and honor of king would elevate him to much too high a position. The fact that two divergent accounts have been joined together in this report of the origin of kingship speaks for the accuracy and reliability of the biblical narrative at this point. In the one account, kingship is advocated; in the other, it is clearly opposed. When one reads Chapters 8 through 12 of First Samuel, contradictions become apparent. According to one emphasis, King Saul was jubilantly celebrated as a deliverer sent from God in time of distress. According to the other, the cry for a king was regarded as showing disrespect for God, and the dangers which kingship held for the people of God were pointed out.

A superficial evaluation might stop with the identifying of the contradiction and conclude that one account must be false. However, upon closer observation it is clear that this apparent contradiction points to the important historical circumstance that there were actually two opposing lines of thought in Israel at the time kingship was being established. This conflict continued throughout the history of kingship and long thereafter. Traces of this are still evident in the crucifixion of Jesus and in the process which led to it. One need only recall the words above the cross (Matt. 27:37).

After the tragic death of Saul, the first of Israel's kings, kingship blossomed for a brief period under David and his successor. During this time it enjoyed expansion, splendor, and good fortune. Through the prophet Nathan, David's dynasty received a great promise from God. In Second Samuel 7 we read:

*"When your days are fulfilled and you lie down with your
fathers, I will raise up your descendant,[3]
And I will establish his kingdom . .
I will be a father to him, and he shall be a son to me [4]
. . . And your house and your kingdom shall be made sure for-
ever. . . . "* (vv. 12-16)

This promise holds the key to the question of why the history of
kingship in Israel has a place in the Bible at all. It is reported in
the Bible because here a portion of political history was introduced
and determined by a word of God. However, we must also point
out that this is reported from the end of this history, from the
shocking realization that the kings had failed and that the nation
which had been given such an exalted promise for its kingdom had
failed.

The so-called deuteronomic history, which sums up the entire
history of the kings, originated during the Exile under the direct
influence of the collapse of the kingdom. Here something unusual
took place: A people, through the annihilation of its political existence, developed a concept of its overall history in terms of a confession of guilt. There is a pronounced relationship between the
two major works into which the history of Israel was compiled.
The nucleus of the Pentateuch, which presents Israel's early history, consists of a confession of praise for God's act of deliverance
at the beginning of Israel's history. The fundamental motif of the
deuteronomic history, which comprises Israel's later history as a
nation, consists of a confession of guilt. Moreover, the latter attrib-
utes to the kings a great deal of the responsibility for what had
taken place.

The above conclusion is not self-evident. When we read this history today we are more likely to ask how the actual history of the
Israelite monarchy can be reconciled with the promise we find at
its beginning. In contrast to what God had promised David and his
dynasty, the actual course of history shows a step-by-step decline
of the monarchy from the lofty heights it had enjoyed only under
David and Solomon. From this we might conclude that the promise

---

[3] Translator's Note: Here the RSV reads, "I will raise up your son after you,
who shall come forth from your body."
[4] Translator's Note: Here the RSV reads, "I will be his father, and he shall be
my son."

was questionable. In Israel's history-writing, the opposite conclusion was drawn; the reason for the deepening contrast between the history of the monarchy and the promise was seen in the fact that the kings did not take the promise as seriously as it had been intended. The kings no longer officially recognized their ties with God's directives.

What a faith that must have been to have held firmly to a promise given to the house of David in the face of a historical development which spanned centuries and which was clearly moving in the opposite direction! In this faith we can see the roots of the messianic expectation, the awaiting of another king who in later times was called the Messiah, the Anointed One. This name, which in the Greek form, "Christ," was applied to Jesus of Nazareth, gives the clearest expression of the relationship of kingship to God. Through the rite of anointment God bestowed upon the king those qualifications necessary for his office. When the followers of Jesus acknowledged him as the Christ, they were referring to the history of a promise which had met failure among the kings, which gradually had been transformed in the expectation of the people, and which now in the person of Jesus was reaching its fulfillment.

The promise given to the house of David was not God's only word on kingship, however. From the beginning there also appeared the prophets' message of judgment, God's "no" to the kings who turned away from him. The sharp contradiction between this "no" and the "yes" of the promise concerning kingship became history in the recurring conflicts between prophets and kings which grew more acute until the prophets finally were persecuted and, in some instances, even put to death. At the end of this process stands the account of Jeremiah's suffering and the figure of the suffering servant of God, about whom the prophet of the Exile speaks (cf. Isa. 42:104, 49:1-6, 50:4-9, 52:13–53:12). This line of prophecy led to a fulfillment proclaimed in the New Testament—Jesus of Nazareth was the suffering servant of God in whom the history of prophecy reached its goal.

Against this background it becomes understandable that the early Christian community saw in Jesus the awaited king of Israel, the Messiah, as well as the suffering servant. The manner in which the lines of kingship and prophecy converge in the person of Jesus is reflected in his dialogue with Pilate, as recorded in the passion history of John's Gospel. To Pilate's question, "So you are a king?" Jesus replied:

> *"You say that I am a king.*
> *For this I was born, and for this I have come into the world*
> *to bear witness to the truth."*

(John 18:37)

These two statements simply do not fit together: A king's primary function is not "to bear witness to the truth," but in Jesus the office of prophet and the transformed office of king were again united, and in his passion he executed this reunified office.

The idea of the kingly rule of God was current in Israel apart from any reference to the rule of earthly kings or the expectation of a coming Messiah. In late Judaism we encounter this concept in two common expressions. It was common to speak of "taking upon oneself the yoke of the kingdom of God," which simply meant to recognize God as sovereign.[5] However, since this was understood to be a free decision, this expression tacitly presupposed that God did not exercise his kingship in such a manner that he forced everyone to bow down before him. This points to the other expression which occurs in the frequently expressed petition pleading for the manifestation of God's kingly rule.[6]

The proclamation of Jesus attached itself directly to this expectation of the reign of God, as expressed in this petition. It was to this expectation that he was referring in his parables of the kingdom of heaven, or of the kingly rule of God. At the same time, Jesus must have deeply disappointed this expectation, and the Gospels clearly reflect this. The essential offense, as far as the religious leaders of his day were concerned, rested in the fact that Jesus associated the manifestation of God's kingly rule with his own activity,

---

[5] Translator's Note: e.g. reciting the first section of the *Shema* (Deut. 6:4-9), and thus acknowledging the One God, was called: "to take upon oneself the yoke of the kingdom of heaven." Tanhuma Yeh leka I, f. 24a, or "Take upon you the yoke of the kingdom of heaven, and excel one another in the fear of God, and do deeds of lovingkindness one towards the other." *Sifre Deut.*, Ha'azinu 323, f. 138b. Cf. also Matt. 11:30, Jer. 5:5, Lam. 3:27, Ecclus. 51:26.

[6] Translator's Note: The Kaddish, which pious Jews prayed in the time of Jesus, as they do today, closes with this petition: "May he establish his kingdom during your life and during your days, and during the life of all the house of Israel."

thus uniting in himself two sharply contrasting lines of thought, the one centering around the kingship of God, the other around the awaited Messiah. Whether or not Jesus designated himself as the Messiah never has become really clear, nor has it become clear what he intended by designating himself as the "son of man."

When one surveys the process which led to the concept of the kingly rule of God in the parables of Jesus as well as to the name "Christ," it becomes clear how inseparably the message of Christ is bound up with the history out of which it arose. It also becomes clear that the realm of the political had been assimilated into this message, not in the sense that Jesus' message had even the slightest political character, but indeed in the sense that through the fulfillment of an expectation which originally had political implications, whatever significance the political realm might have had for salvation had come to an end once and for all.

Chapter XVIII

The Proof of Prophecy

In the New Testament we frequently encounter the expression, "as it is written" or, "All this took place to fulfill what the Lord had spoken by the prophet . . . " (Matt. 1:22). This frequent reference from the New Testament to the Old Testament is called prophetic or scriptural proof. These scriptural proof texts present a special stumbling-block to anyone who today attempts to understand the Bible. The manner in which individual Old Testament passages are taken out of context and are brought into the argument appears incomprehensible to our way of thinking and an explanation is necessary. Let us begin with a familiar example.

The account of John the Baptist's call to repentance is introduced with these words,

> *For this is he who was spoken of by the prophet Isaiah when he said:*
>> *"The voice of one crying in the wilderness:*
>> *Prepare the way of the Lord,*
>> *Make his paths straight."*

(Matt. 3:3)

Here John the Baptist is described as the one who prepares the way, and it is asserted that the Prophet Isaiah had announced John's coming. In its original context, the passage quoted reads: "A voice cries [or the voice of one crying]: 'In the wilderness prepare the way of the Lord . . . '" (Isa. 40:3a). Here it is not a man who is calling but a heavenly servant of God. The voice transmits the command from God that a way shall be prepared over which the

97

Israelites exiled in Babylonia can return to their homeland. Thus, in its original context, the passage has an entirely different meaning from that given it in the report concerning John the Baptist. This same phenomenon can be pointed out in a great many of the so-called proof passages in which an Old Testament quotation is used to support a New Testament occurrence.

Here we must concede that this type of prophetic proof is no longer valid in understanding the Bible. Whenever this text is used for an Advent sermon, it must be made clear that, according to our understanding, the statement from the Book of Isaiah has a meaning quite different from that given it by Matthew. We must further add that it is not the eighth century (B.C.) Prophet Isaiah who is speaking here; it is the unknown prophet of the Exile whom we call Deutero-Isaiah.[1]

Permit me to cite one example from Paul: In the fourteenth chapter of his First Letter to the Corinthians, Paul concludes on the basis of a passage from the Prophet Isaiah that speaking in tongues applies not to believers but to unbelievers (14:21 f.). The passage reads: "By men of strange tongues and by the lips of foreigners will I speak to this people, and even then they will not listen to me. . . . " In its original context, this passage meant that the people of Israel were being informed that they would be oppressed by nations with languages foreign to them (cf. Isa. 28:11-13). Here again the Old Testament passage in its original context has a meaning quite different from that given it by Paul.

If such quotations are no longer able to provide conclusive evidence, it is due to the change in our understanding of or relationship to history. We no longer think in any way except in terms of historical distances and historical relationships, hence we can hear such a statement from the Old Testament only in terms of its original meaning. This also applies when we read the Bible. For Paul and Matthew and the other New Testament writers, such historical reflection did not exist; when confronted with an Old Testament passage, they did not ask what it meant when first spoken. We can only state this as a fact, which was by no means true only of the Bible; rather, this was true of the entire period in which it was common to think in this way. The manner in which Philo of Alex-

---

[1] Translator's Note on page 15.

andria, a learned Jewish author from around the year 40 A.D.,[2] quotes Scripture departs still farther from the original meaning of the passages he quotes.

It would also be of no help in understanding the scriptural proof used in the New Testament if we were to push into the background the fact that such proofs are no longer valid for us today and were then to salvage as many of these passages as possible. In these prophetic proof texts we are not dealing with proclamation but with supporting the proclamation by a method valid for that period.

Now we can inquire into the positive significance of the Old Testament quotations in the New Testament. This significance can best be viewed from the perspective of an entirely different method of quoting Old Testament passages which, by the way, were not intended to serve as scriptural proof texts. Here one must separate the predictions of the Old Testament from the promises of a coming Savior. It is not until the New Testament that the predictions discussed above appeared as predictions of this type. The promises, on the other hand, arose out of the moment in which they were issued, out of the passionate waiting of a people that had walked in darkness, out of the oppressive experiences of suffering and guilt, out of the hope that God once again would turn to his people.

The promises of a coming Redeemer assumed diverse forms in the Old Testament and can be understood in various ways. From the New Testament we know that at the time of Jesus many people, on the basis of these promises, expected a political Messiah. The New Testament tells us that these many promises need not all be interpreted as having reference to Christ. Furthermore, these promises did not possess then, any more than they do today, the power to relieve anyone of the decision of faith. They all expressed the fact that God's dealing with his people was not completed with the closing of the Old Testament. The series of promises interwoven throughout the Old Testament were a moving element in the history

---

[2] Translator's Note: Philo was a Jewish philosopher who distinguished himself in intellectual circles as the first thinker to intimately join rational philosophy and the revealed religion of the Jews. His long treatises attempt to spiritualize the laws and narratives of the Old Testament and by means of fanciful interpretations make them say the same thing as the religious philosophers of his day.

of Israel where even in moments of deepest despair the waiting for a new reality never ceased.

In the fourth chapter of the Gospel according to Luke the beginning of Jesus' ministry is portrayed in this manner: Jesus enters the synagogue in his hometown, Nazareth, and reads a portion from the Prophet Isaiah where it is written:

> *"The Spirit of the Lord is upon me, because he has anointed me;*
> *he has sent me to preach the Gospel to the poor,*
> *to bind up the brokenhearted . . . "* (v. 18).[3]

He then lays the scroll aside and says: "Today this scripture has been fulfilled in your hearing" (v. 21). In this account the real significance of the Old Testament for Jesus, as well as for the early Christian community, becomes clear. There was no attempt to prove something by means of statements from the Old Testament; rather, it was asserted that what had been announced in the prophecy of the Old Testament, the coming of the age of salvation, had arrived.

The same thing was expressed in Jesus' reply to John the Baptist (Matt. 11:2-6). In this sense, Jesus was referring to the same announcement of the age of salvation when he asserted that this was now a reality. In both instances it was clear that this claim met with opposition, encountered doubt, and became controversial.

In these instances it is not just any arbitrary Old Testament statement but the heart of the Old Testament's prophetic message of salvation that is applied to the activity of Jesus. It is entirely reasonable to apply such promises to the activity of Jesus, based on our historical understanding of the original context of the passages quoted. One could cite a whole series of other instances in the New Testament where the same thing is true of the manner in which Old Testament texts are quoted. In 2 Corinthians, Chapter 6, Paul quotes from Deutero-Isaiah:

> *"In a time of favor* [4] *I have listened to you,*
> *and helped you on the day of salvation."*
> (2 Cor. 6:2, cf. Isa. 49:8)

---

[3] Translator's Note: This is a translation of the author's own rendering of Luke 4:18. Note especially that, unlike the RSV, the author has included "to bind up the brokenhearted," which is found in some Greek manuscripts as well as in Isaiah 61:1-2, the Old Testament passage from which Jesus is here quoting.

He then adds: "Behold now is the time of favor,[4] behold, now is the day of salvation." Elsewhere Paul summarizes the same thoughts when he says: "For all the promises of God find their 'Yes' in him. That is why we utter the Amen through him . . . " (2 Cor. 1:20).

In the New Testament *all* quoting of Old Testament passages was based on the claim that the promises of God from the old covenant were fulfilled in Christ. Therefore the prophecies are not used as proof texts in the strictest sense of the term, not even in the New Testament. If they were, the confession of Jesus as the Christ no longer would be made on the basis of faith alone. In other words, here one should not speak in terms of prophetic proof at all. The fact that Jesus had ushered in the age of salvation which had been proclaimed in the Old Testament could not be proved by any means whatsoever, not even by means of the Old Testament.

Only by recognizing this limitation will we be able to view in perspective the constant attempt to relate to the Old Testament what was happening to Christ's followers through him. For the New Testament, the activity, the discourses, and the suffering of Jesus Christ are part of a greater, more comprehensive history, and it is for this reason that connecting lines are constantly being drawn back to the Old Testament. Only on the surface does it appear as though the emphasis were on the fact that what was taking place had been predicted by someone in the past, and that it is thereby verified. What is essential rests beneath the surface: The fact that each time a passage from the Old Testament is quoted, a history is being quoted, which extends from the Beginning to the End.

Whenever someone confesses Jesus as the Christ, he enters this history, which did not end with the fulfillment in Christ. The rule of God, ushered in at Christ's coming, is not yet evident to everyone; thus time, hastening toward fulfillment, goes on. The history of the church in the world, a history beginning with the coming of Christ, corresponds to the history which led to Christ. For Christianity, also, the time of waiting has not come to an end; she, too, utters the petition: "Thy kingdom come!"

Herein lies the real easing of the tension between the Old and

---

[4] Translator's Note: Here the RSV reads, "the acceptable time" instead of "a time of favor." Cf. this passage as translated in the *New English Bible*.

the New Testament message—the fact that in both instances the word of God possesses the amazing capacity to span vast historical distances and to take a man, or group of men, at his place in history and place him at the heart of an occurrence which has such a far-reaching impact. That is the meaning of those Old Testament statements which point beyond their own boundaries to something and someone still to come. That is also the meaning of the New Testament statements in which the present and the future became deeply anchored in the history of God's activity from the Beginning on.

Chapter XIX

Messengers of Christ
and the Essence of Mission

At the beginning of this book we discussed the essence of God's message. We observed how the Gospels came into being as the message made its way into the world, how the prophets of the Old Testament received the word of God and transmitted it as the word of a messenger. At the heart of both the Old and New Testaments, the spokesmen of that word, the prophets and the apostles, were messengers.

When we speak of message in this context, we are thinking of the mission carried out by the apostles of Jesus Christ, as reported in the Book of Acts, and mission as an undertaking of the churches today. This brings us again to a point of controversy: The mission endeavor of the church today is being seriously questioned by many, and there is growing opposition to the Christian mission in lands where the church traditionally has carried on foreign mission work. At the same time there is a growing recognition of the fact that the Christian church must assume a much stronger missionary character. These contradictory points of view could indicate that we are in the midst of a change in the traditional understanding of mission; they could be the indication of a renewal.

When looking through the Book of Acts to see what it has to report concerning the movement of the message of Christ into the world, the reader is struck by what little ado is made over this movement. Soberly, calmly, and without emotion, the story is told of how the message moved from city to city and province to province, how one congregation after another came into being in Syria, Asia Minor, Greece, and Rome. Not the slightest attempt is made to view the spread of Christianity from the viewpoint of human achievement. In dealing with the apostles, as well as in speaking of the congregations, the Book of Acts has almost more negative than positive things to say about human capabilities and achievements. In a manner hardly conceivable to us today, human planning and organization receded into the background as the Gospel made its way into the world.

This indicates from a negative viewpoint the moving force of mission in primitive Christianity. Here was a movement propelled by a force moving from a totally different dimension into the realm of history, a movement into which people threw themselves as into a swift current. Perhaps this will become clearer if I point to a parallel which shows how the messengers of both the Old and New Testament, seized and driven by the same force, had to do what they did and say what they said. The apostles, when commanded not to speak at all, answered: "For we cannot but speak of what we have seen and heard" (Acts 4:20). And the Prophet Amos, also told not to speak, said:

> "The lion has roared;
>   who will fear?
> The Lord God has spoken;
>   who can but prophesy?"
>
> (Amos 3:8)

In both instances it is the same directness which opens the way for the word.

However, with the allusion to this force at work among the messengers we have not sufficiently clarified the concept of mission. In the old covenant, prophecy was limited to a definite period of time. The call of a messenger of God was in answer to a specific historical moment, to a definite situation. It was no different in the case of the messengers of Jesus Christ in the New Testament. The coming of Christ, the moment of fulfillment, had a direct effect on the movement of his message into the world. In the Book of Acts it is evident to what a great extent the existence of mission is based on this historical moment. What is reported is not a gradual advance in the undertaking of mission but a breakthrough of something entirely new, without precedent, which the witnesses could only perceive in amazement as they themselves were drawn into the movement.

First of all, there was the Pentecost event (Acts 2). Here the message of the Christ broke through in the languages of the then known world. This can be understood only against the background of what the story of the Tower of Babel attempts to say (Gen. 11:1-9). This old story, originating out of the realm of mythology, speaks of the lack of understanding which plagues human beings divided by language. This narrative directly precedes the promise to Abraham, which declares: "In you all the families of the earth shall be blessed" (Gen. 12:3).

When the nations of the Mediterranean world are listed in the Pentecost account—the Parthians and Medes and Elamites, etc.— this old promise certainly is called to mind. When the residents of these various nations, under the influence of the apostles' preaching, declared: "We hear them telling in our own tongues the mighty works of God," they were expressing their amazement over a miracle in which they saw that in the message about Christ a word capable of breaking through the boundaries of language was making its way into the world.

Insofar as this miracle took place through the speaking of ordinary men, it was also these men who were affected by the miracle. That is what the outpouring of the Holy Spirit was attempting to say. In current explanations, this part of the Pentecost account usually is presented in such a vague and incredible manner that the festival of Pentecost has almost lost its real significance. Nothing was intended by the word "spirit" except that force or power from God which suddenly overtakes a man and which never can be measured in human terms. The accompanying phenomena, however—the rush of the mighty wind and the tongues of fire—are related to God's appearances of old. Both of these, the charisma, or extraordinary power, which seizes a man and the manifestation of God to his people, belong to the early traditions of Israel. In the same manner in which the spirit of God bestowed upon a simple man the capacity to arise as the deliverer of his people, the spirit now enabled the apostles in their simple manner of speaking to pierce the divisive boundaries of languages. As God appeared to his people then, he came now to the little band of disciples and gave their words the power to open the way for the message.

The second breakthrough also appears in the Book of Acts, in a scarcely noticed narrative about the conversion of Cornelius (Acts 10), the Roman centurion who sent for Peter. While the servants of Cornelius were on their way to get him, Peter had a strange vision in which he was commanded to kill unclean animals and eat them, but he resisted this command by saying: "... I have never eaten anything that is common or unclean." He received the answer: "What God has cleansed, you must not call common." He later explained the vision in this manner: "God has shown me that I should not call any man common or unclean."

This narrative shows that Peter, even as a Christian missionary, still accepted the old Jewish distinction between clean and unclean. Here we have an idea of what the break with these regulations concerning purification must have meant for the early Christian community. To live with, to eat with, and to keep close company with Gentile Christians was possible only through lifting the regulations concerning purification, which indeed had regulated everyday life from morning to evening. It was a historical moment when this centuries-old barrier fell because Christ had come for the Gentiles as well as for the Jews. This breakthrough manifested something of what we call humanity. This is beautifully expressed in the story of Cornelius who wanted to fall down at Peter's feet because he saw in him something that was godlike; but Peter lifted him up and said to him: "Stand up; I too am a man."

The third breakthrough is found in the conversion of Paul (Acts 9), whose missionary activity determines the entire second part of the Book of Acts. The significance of this breakthrough rests in the fact that Paul, a theologian, a man who was a leader in the Judaism of that day, acknowledged Jesus as the Messiah, the Christ, and placed his life in his service. In Paul were united the qualities of intellectual leadership and personal devotion. He was with equal passion both theologian and missionary; but in both positions he was a servant of Christ, so that his life represented continuous affliction and trouble without his ever receiving honor and recognition from his fellowmen, without his ever enjoying some of the fruits of his tireless efforts, without his ever finding among his own congregations the response which, at least from a human point of view, would have made his service easier.

Western theology has not given sufficient attention to this connection between Paul's missionary service and what he says in his letters to the various congregations. He was not a theologian in the sense that we understand this today. He had no teaching position. We therefore should not abstract a teaching from those things which he says in his letters to the congregations. His position was one of mission; for him, teaching had only the secondary function of serving in the proclamation of the message. The reference to Paul's conversion in the Book of Acts describes a turning to Christ within the framework of Jewish theology which otherwise had almost totally rejected the Christian message. However, in Paul, turning to Christ took the form of missionary activity in which he endured suffering, persecution, and grave dangers (2 Cor. 11:16-33).

When we see in Paul not only a theologian but also a missionary, it must be clear that Paul stands closer to the prophets than is usually realized. Just as we can gain little understanding of the prophets if we observe only what they said without at the same time observing the fact that they were speaking as messengers, so we can gain little understanding of who Paul was if we detach his theology from his missionary service.

In one of his laments, Jeremiah said: "I sat alone, because thy hand was upon me" (Jer. 15:17). Paul could have said something quite similar, and perhaps he did. Freedom from the law, the freedom in Christ which releases one from the statutes of the Mosaic law, a freedom which Paul in his letters so tirelessly proclaimed as the essential breakthrough of the new creature, had in Paul's own life little resemblance to what we usually understand as freedom.

Once, in coming to terms with his opponents in Corinth, Paul spoke of the hardships of his service: "Are they servants of Christ? I am a better one—I am talking like a madman—with far greater labors, far more imprisonments, with countless beatings, and often near death . . . " (2 Cor. 11:23). This is followed by a long list of afflictions he had endured in his service, a list which is downright shocking to read. When one questions why such a burden should have been imposed upon one individual, the only answer is the one Paul himself received from the Lord when he besought him to remove a severe affliction from him: " . . . my power is made perfect in weakness" (2 Cor. 12:9).

This was the same power that gave the prophets the courage to follow their lonesome course when they were called to their unique positions of messengers of God. What took place in Paul's missionary service was not unique to or even typical of Christianity. It was instead an unusual occurrence bound up with the unique moment of the Gospel's breakthrough into the broad expanse of the Roman Empire.

We have reflected upon the three breakthroughs which determined the course of the Book of Acts and have discovered the direction we should follow in seeking an answer to the question concerning mission. Mission always has to do with such breakthroughs; in an established church they show that God is on the move with his people and that these advances into new areas are bound up with that power which is mighty in weakness.

Chapter XX

The Canon of Holy Scriptures

I recently heard of a pastor who brought a Hebrew Old Testament and a Greek New Testament with him to confirmation instruction in order to show the students the original form of both Testaments. This brought forth an astonished exclamation from one of them: "Does that mean that the original text of the Bible never existed as *one* book?" The idea of Holy Scriptures as one continuous book has been so impressed upon our minds that it can be startling to learn that there never was *one* original Bible in *one* original language. The first complete Bibles were the Greek manuscripts from early Christian times containing the Old Testament translated from Hebrew into Greek, in addition to the New Testament in its original Greek.

Both parts of the Bible originated from individual books or writings which once existed by themselves and were read and circulated independently. Through the discovery of the writings in the caves of Qumran by the Dead Sea, it has clearly been demonstrated to us how the Isaiah scroll found there was the same as the scrolls kept in the synagogues of Nazareth and Capernaum when Jesus read from one of them (cf. Luke 4:16 ff.). When all books were in the form of scrolls, it was impossible, from a practical point of view, to have, for instance, the entire Old Testament on one scroll. Consequently, until the time of Jesus, the Old Testament existed only in individual volumes or scrolls. For the people of that time it was not one book but a library, a collection of books.

This was no different in the case of the New Testament. The

Gospels existed for a long time as individual writings, and the Epistles at first were circulated only among the congregations or groups within the congregations, to which they had been directed. The essential difference was that the Old Testament as such did not come into being until the end of the history of God's people of the old covenant. It gradually took form over the course of about a thousand years, and not until the last two centuries before Christ was it considered a closed entity. The New Testament, however, originated at the beginning of the history of God's people of the new covenant, within the course of about a century. Since then, almost 2,000 years of church history have passed during which the Bible has remained unchanged. It is understandable that the weight of this history should have led to an understanding of the Bible which no longer was conscious of the gradual growth of the collection and the diverse origin of the various books.

So long as the Bible enjoyed undisputed acceptance within the realm of western civilization, questions concerning the formation and limiting of the canon never arose, or interested only those with special theological training. However, when the Bible becomes the center of controversy, the question concerning the canon takes on special importance.

The fact that the Old Testament alone was the Bible of Christendom for several generations is scarcely known today. The Old Testament was not only Jesus' Bible, it was also the Bible of the primitive church. Aside from the Old Testament, the only other authoritative sources at first were the sayings of Jesus himself, and these existed only in the form of oral traditions. Thus Christianity has learned from the Old Testament what Holy Scripture is and what it means. In order to emphasize his point, even Luther stated that it would be sufficient if the church possessed only the Old Testament, that the New Testament has its true existence in the oral transmission and indeed as proclamation, and that the message was put into written form only as a matter of expediency.[1] This is in complete accord with the fact that the early Christian congrega-

---

[1] These thoughts were expressed in an Epiphany sermon on the text of Matthew 2:1-12, *D. Martin Luthers Werke*, Vol. 10:1 (Weimar: Herman Bohlaus Nachfolger, 1910), pp. 625-627, or *The Precious and Sacred Writings of Martin Luther*, Vol. 10 (Church Postil: Gospels), John N. Lenken, ed. (Minneapolis: Lutherans in All Lands Co., 1905), pp. 371-373.

tions managed for a considerable period of time without a fixed canon of scriptures which were authoritative within the church, as well as with the fact that the impetus for putting the New Testament message into written form did not arise from any inner need of the congregations.

It was, above all, the attempt of Marcion (a Christian shipping magnate who lived about 150 A.D. and who organized a congregation of his own) to gather together a fixed collection of Christian documents that made it necessary for the church to establish a fixed list of those writings which she considered authoritative. Marcion had attempted to exclude the Old Testament from the Christian church and to eliminate from those writings of the New Testament which already were widely accepted at that time everything which appeared to him to have an Old Testament flavor. In coming to terms with the direction taken by Marcion, as well as with other groups which also were deviating from her teaching, the church gradually, in several stages extending over a long period of time, arrived at the New Testament as we have it today. This, however, did not take place until after a long struggle which had its effect upon the entire church of that day. The authority of several books, such as the Revelation to John and some of the shorter Epistles, continued to be disputed for a long time. The final acceptance of the New Testament with its present content did not take place in either the eastern or the western church until about 400 A.D.

The fact that the authority of a good number of writings found in the New Testament could be disputed as late as 400 A.D., even by some of the church's leading theologians, while other writings such as I Clement [2] were considered as canonical or authoritative in some parts of the church, is a warning against a torpid concept of canonicity. Of more importance, however, were the conflicts over the validity of certain writings. These conflicts were possible

---

[2] Translator's Note: I Clement is a letter ascribed by tradition to Clement, reputedly a disciple of Peter and third bishop of Rome, and sent around 95 A.D. as an official communication from the church in Rome to the Church in Corinth. The letter attempts to help settle some disputes over leadership which had arisen within the Corinthian church. Codex Alexandrinus, an important fifth century manuscript, includes I Clement among the writings of the New Testament.

only because of the existence of fixed criteria for determining canonicity. The two basic factors which determined the formation of the canon remained fixed from the very beginning and never were tampered with in all these conflicts over individual books. When people spoke of the canon, it was with these two principal elements in mind: "the Lord," that is, the sayings of the Lord, and "the apostles," that is, the writings of the apostles.

With this basing of the canon upon the Lord and the apostles, it was clear, in spite of differences in detail, that the New Testament was the foundation and plumbline of the church's faith. It contained the message of Christ as received from the mouths of witnesses. From the beginning it was not a teaching or a set of ideas which was considered to be the heart of the New Testament; it was the witness to Christ. Here there is complete agreement between the criteria used in arriving at the authentic canon of New Testament writings and those used in the preaching of the apostles, as well as in the earliest and simplest confessions of the primitive church. There are no other criteria for determining what belongs in the New Testament except the heart of the New Testament itself as it existed in the proclamation of the church and the declaration of faith in him before any literary fixation took place.

Further support for this can be found in a proceeding which occurred during the formation of the Old Testament. The Old Testament's major historical works grew entirely out of the confession of God's acts, especially the confession of praise expressed by those who had been delivered at the beginning of Israel's history and the confession of guilt rendered after the collapse of the kingdom by those who had been brought to their defeat by God. Now, since the history of the formation of the Old Testament extends over many centuries, this relationship is spelled out with much more detail and variety than is the case in the New Testament, and we have a much clearer picture of the interaction between the history of worship and the growth of the Bible. We see this already in the Ten Commandments, which had their "situation in life" in a cultic ceremony, and in the original confession of those rescued at the Reed Sea, which took the form of a divine eulogy.[3] It continues in

---

[3] Translator's Note: Here the author is referring to the Song of Miriam (Ex. 15:21), considered among the oldest traditions in the Old Testament.

the fixed creeds which summarize the most important salvation events of the early period,[4] and even in certain Psalms [5] which in prayer or hymn form list the same series of events that we find portrayed in the historical books. This all indicates how the Bible grew out of the living drama of worship.

In like manner, recent New Testament research has discovered in both the Epistles and the Gospels traces of various elements of worship—hymns and prayers of the early Christian community, the earliest creeds, and portions of the preaching and instruction of the early congregations.

Thus the earlier conception of the canon of biblical writings has undergone a fundamental change. The process by which the canon was finally fixed and limited now appears as a conclusion which brought about little change in the actual development of the Bible. Rather, the actual development of the Bible took place among the people of God as they lived out their existence between God and the world, along the course over which God led them. This applies to the entire Bible, both Old and New Testament.

This is of vital significance for our present-day inquiry concerning the canon, its boundaries and substance. It is now clear that the purely theoretical approach to the question—that is, the approach which seeks to determine which books of the Old and New Testaments are perhaps not fully entitled to a place within the Bible, or whether there are other books which should have a place in it—cannot determine the position of the church toward the canon, or rather, the position of the canon within the church. That such questions are raised from time to time can only have a healing effect. The essential question, however, is how the Bible, as it has been handed down to us, lives within the church and what the Bible through the church conveys to the world.

When we observe the living effect of the Bible within the church, we come to the natural conclusion that the Bible is in constant motion within the history of the church. It is entirely in order that the emphasis in the church's proclamation, teaching, and worship

---

[4] Translator's Note: Here reference is being made to the short historical credos such as, Deut. 6:20-24 and 26:5b-9, also considered among the older traditions in the Old Testament and also having a cultic origin (cf. above pp. 29, 30, 33).
[5] Translator's Note: Compare the events listed in the creed in Deuteronomy 26:5b-9 to Psalm 136:10-22, 135:8-11, etc.

should change from one part of the Bible to another. That one part of the Bible which for a long time had been silent should be rediscovered and make its message heard while other parts which automatically had been considered as the most important recede into the background is all part of the course which God traverses with his church. We now are experiencing the fact that many parts of the Old Testament once again are speaking forth in an entirely new and vital manner. In the difficult years just past, the Revelation to John, which long had remained silent, suddenly was heard once again. These are good signs of the vital interaction between the Bible and the people of God.

Another example illustrates this fact even more clearly. For a long time the church, in her practice as well as in her interpretation, listened to the psalms so one-sidedly that it appeared as though only a few of them, above all the psalms of trust, still spoke to man in a direct manner. In the violent upheavals of the past decade, many congregations and many individuals have experienced, independently from each other, the fact that the Psalter again has awakened to a totally new life.

These various experiences with the Bible are in complete accord with its origins. Because it presents the history of God's dealing with his people and because even today that history is still moving toward a goal, the Bible still is a living book. Until the goal is reached which the Creator has set for his creation, the Bible will remain inexhaustible. So long as we remain pilgrims, there is for us no conclusive, no final and closed interpretation of the Bible. We must remain inquirers so long as we have not reached the goal. The authority of the Bible is the authority of the living God. The work of interpretation, the question concerning the formation of the writings in the Bible, the searching for those overlapping themes and connecting links which give unity to the Bible, and the wrestling with the difficulties which are encountered by each interpretation all point from the controversial Bible to the living Word which was in the Beginning, which shall be at the End, and which at the midpoint in time became man.

Chapter XXI

Concerning One's Personal
Approach to the Bible

With this chapter we shall close our discussion of the controversial Bible by stating several points which are intended to be of assistance in one's personal approach to the Bible. While the essays in this book were taking form, it often occurred to me how difficult it must be for anyone not versed in theology to discover the meaning of biblical statements, see the broader as well as the more immediate contexts, and understand what had been spoken so long ago in terms of its significance for our present time. At this point it is not especially comforting to realize that theologians apparently are not in a much better position, otherwise their interpretations of the Bible would reflect more agreement and be more easily understood. Yet, even the most lucid and widely recognized interpretation of the Bible cannot change the fact that the Bible reaches centuries into the past and that it therefore can never be as accessible to us as a religious book written in the language of our own times.

Here we once again must raise the question: Why does the Bible project over this enormous interval of time up to our present day, why has no opposition, no indifference been able to silence it? Why do people still make an effort to understand it? The answer to these questions is clear; it simply rests in the fact that the chain of those confronted by the living God through the words of this book has never been broken.

The Bible has a focal point in the report concerning the man Jesus of Nazareth, through whom God revealed his disposition toward mankind. The Bible continues to be handed on in order that it may continue the message that God has turned himself in love toward all mankind. This is the ultimate concern of the Bible and it is this which sets the clear and simple tenor of the entire Bible. Since this often is difficult to believe in view of the reality of our own existence and the course of world history, the Bible is at many points a most difficult book, not easily understood. It is for this reason that the Bible is controversial.

The basic prerequisite for a personal approach to the Bible rests in the fact that everyone who opens its pages should question it in terms of his own life. Only thus can there be an encounter between the reader, the Bible, and what the Bible really attempts to be— the living word of God. The heart of the Bible states that God has turned himself to man just as man really is, with his worldly ideas, his day-to-day needs, his laughing and crying, his relationship to his surroundings. For a personal approach to the Bible, it is basic that we constantly encounter the Bible anew, that out of our own lives questions arise which we then direct to the Bible, that as the result of some new experience we hear a portion of the Bible in a new fashion, that we learn to view our personal surroundings within the broader context of the Bible, that what apparently is meaningless takes on meaning, and finally that within the perspective of the biblical drama our own finitude is brought into relationship with the infinite.

If we listen to the Bible and out of our own human experience direct questions to it, unexpected access to the Bible will be opened to us. We will then notice that the persons who speak and act in the Bible are much like us in that they, too, usually are not models of piety at all and by no means always immediately believe everything God says. We will discover that the great acts of God reported in the Bible do not always encounter the appropriate human counterpart, but encounter failure, indecision, and egoism, too. It will then become clear to us that the Bible also shares in the brokenness of human existence and in this way bears witness to the fact that God has accepted us just as we are. The Bible can speak to us because in it God's word comes to us in the form of a book written by men and bound by the limitations of human existence.

If we understand this, we will no longer attempt to comprehend the entire Bible all at once. The Bible can address us with just *one* word at any given time, and it is filled with words and stories easily understood without need of any explanatory remarks. If anyone is really serious about hearing a word from God addressed to his specific situation, receiving an answer to a particular question, or understanding the direction in which he should go, he will not open the Bible in vain.

There is something else involved here. To be able to open the Bible and read in it a word directed to his situation, a person must first have some idea where to look. The Bible is like a large, densely-wooded forest; one must know something about the paths which lead into it. If the Bible is to have the opportunity to speak, one must have some acquaintance with it, even if that be ever so modest.

For this reason there are always two aspects to a personal approach to the Bible: First, there must be questions arising out of one's own existence and, secondly, there must be persistent growth in one's familiarity with the Bible. In all Christian churches there are two fundamental methods by which the Bible is handed on: proclamation and teaching. In order that the word of God may be imparted, there must be, in addition to worship, the constant work of teaching, from the instruction of children to the teaching of theology in the seminaries. The direct address of God cannot take place apart from the interpretation of the Scriptures, and this task will in turn lose its ultimate meaning without constant reference to the living word of God in the proclamation of the church.

We must acknowledge the fact that the relationship between these two approaches to the Bible—proclamation and teaching—has not always been what it should have been. Scientific theology and ecclesiastical practice have often been too far removed from each other. Theologians, in their research, to some extent lacked sympathy for the task of proclamation, and those who served within the ecclesiastical structure of the church lacked, in part, confidence in the work being carried on by theologians engaged in research. Due to the violent upheavals of our century, the way has been opened for a change, but it will still be a long time before a healthy relationship will again exist between these two methods of transmitting the biblical message.

As comfort for those who suffer the consequences of this cleft between theology and proclamation, it can be said that there are today signs which indicate that the cleft is growing smaller and that there is a growing mutual trust and a readiness to listen to each other. Yet, all this would be to no avail were there not constantly taking place the process described in the parable of the sower (Matt. 13:1 ff.) where, despite all the futility experienced in the sowing, some of the seed falls upon good soil and bears fruit. Without this quiet, unnoticed growth, all activity of the churches and all theological effort would be in vain.

This experience of being moved by a biblical statement and the resulting interest in gaining a clear understanding of the total thrust of the Bible applies also to the average person who listens to the biblical message. With this person in mind, I now will close with a few points which might prove helpful. One can become thoroughly familiar with the Bible only if one reads it in context. At many points in the Bible this is most difficult; at other points it is quite simple. One would do best by beginning with the narrative sections. Here the first step is to read one story entirely, then to read it again and again. One should not immediately try to determine the main point of the story, or extract a teaching from it, or perhaps read into it a deeper meaning. One should approach each story simply as a story and allow it to speak for itself, whether it be the story of the Garden of Eden or the Tower of Babel, the encounter between David and Nathan, the sacrifice of Isaac, or the parable of the prodigal son, the encounter with the disciples on the road to Emmaus, or some other story. Only in this way will one get the feel of the Bible to that point where the Bible will speak entirely of itself.

Here permit me to recall the fact that in the historical books of the Old and New Testaments the Bible speaks a simple, nontheological language which is understandable for everyone who has the patience to listen to it in context. Those who are able to do this will make wonderful discoveries in these simple, yet inexhaustible stories. There are valuable aids available for this purpose. In addition to the King James Version of the Bible, there is the very good and reliable Revised Standard Version. Anyone who can read German or French will benefit by making comparisons with the German *Züricher Bibel* or the French *Bible de Jérusalem* [1] with its excellent introductions and detailed notes. In this comparison with another modern language, one will discover how an ostensibly familiar text can speak with new vitality. A series of commentaries which are reliable from the standpoint of scholarship and easy for the average reader to understand is now available in the *Neue Göttinger Bibelwerk* under the two general titles, "Altes Testament Deutsch" and "Neues Testament Deutsch." [2]

A briefer introduction to all the books of the Bible is offered by *The Layman's Bible Commentary*.[3] Whoever desires further information concerning helps available for Bible study will receive it without difficulty simply by asking someone who is engaged in the exposition of the Bible as part of his profession.

This leads to the last point which I would like to make concerning one's personal approach to the Bible. In our attempt to understand the Bible today we are all compelled to raise questions, regardless of whether we are theological professors, pastors, or laymen. The time has passed when certain people commanded a knowledge of the Bible while others simply allowed this knowledge to pass them by. When it comes to the Bible we all must be inquirers. For this reason it is urgently necessary that we allow room for questions, whether within a congregation, in conferences and other gatherings, or in our personal lives. The Bible has been given to us in order that it might awaken questions and pave the way for answers which may come in the ensuing discussion. It would give me much joy if I were to discover that many persons with questions concerning the Bible had received through this book the courage to bring these questions into the open in order that the great dialogue of the Bible might come alive in our own discussions along the way.

---

[1] Translator's Note: This outstanding volume is available in an English version. See the Appendix for a listing of this and other modern translations of the Bible.

[2] Translator's Note: Many of the leading volumes in the "Altes Testament Deutsch" series are now available in English translation in *The Old Testament Library*, G. Ernest Wright and others, eds. (Philadelphia: Westminster Press).

[3] Translator's Note: For a list of some of the various aids available for Bible study see the "Selected Bibliography of Bible Helps" in the Appendix.

APPENDIX

A Selected Bibliography of Bible Study Helps for Laymen

In the past decade there has appeared on the market a host of good nontechnical books dealing with the Bible, and it is often most difficult for the layman to find his way through this maze of material in order to select those volumes which will help him make the best use of his reading time. This bibliography with its brief comments is an attempt to be of assistance. It is not exhaustive, but, hopefully, the books it includes are representative of the fine scholarship at work on the Bible today and give an indication of the variety of material available to the layman in a form which is both enlightening and readable. I might also point out that it is amazing how many of the books listed below are finding their way into church and public libraries. These libraries should not be overlooked as a source of good aids to Bible study.

THE TRANSLATOR

MODERN TRANSLATIONS OF THE BIBLE

The Holy Bible: Revised Standard Version, Division of Christian Education, National Council of Churches of Christ in the U.S.A., 1946-1952. Presently the most widely used and generally reliable modern translation of the Bible.

The Jerusalem Bible (gen. ed., Alexander Jones). Garden City, N.Y.: Doubleday, 1966. The English version of the French *Bible de Jérusalem* is referred to by the author on page 118. An excellent modern translation with helpful introductions and detailed notes.

Die Züricher Bibel, Kirchensynode des Kantons Zürich. Zürich: Verlag der Zwingli-Bibel, 1907-1931. This German Bible is noted by the author on page 118.

The New English Bible: New Testament. Oxford & Cambridge: Oxford University Press & Cambridge University Press, 1961. The Old Testament counterpart to this excellent British translation is forthcoming.

The New Testament in Modern English (trans. by J. B. Phillips). New York: Macmillan, 1963. Some portions of the Old Testament are now also available in a lively translation by Dr. Phillips, a recognized British scholar.

The New Catholic Edition of the Holy Bible (American Confraternity Version). New York: Benzinger Bros., 1953. An official Roman Catholic translation based on sound scholarship and in good modern English.

Good News for Modern Man. New York: American Bible Society, 1967. A widely heralded modern translation of the New Testament.

The Cotton Patch Version of Paul's Epistles (trans., Clarence Jordan). New York: Association, 1968. "A colloquial modern translation with a Southern accent, vigorous and fervent for the gospel, unsparing in earthiness, rich in humor," rendered by one well versed in the art of New Testament scholarship.

BIBLE DICTIONARIES

Hastings Bible Dictionary (ed., F. C. Grant and H. H. Rowley). New York: Harper, 1963. A standard one-volume work recently revised under the editorship of two leading biblical scholars.

The Interpreter's Dictionary of the Bible, 4 vols. (ed., G. A. Buttrick and others). New York: Abingdon, 1962. By far the best and most comprehensive Bible dictionary in English, written by a host of eminent scholars.

CONCORDANCES

The Oxford Concise Concordance to the Revised Standard Version of the Holy Bible (ed., Bruce M. Metzger and Isabel M. Metzger). New York: Oxford University Press, 1962.

Nelson's Complete Concordance to the Revised Standard Version Bible (ed., John Ellison). New York: Nelson, 1957.

MAPS AND ATLASES

The Westminster Historical Atlas to the Bible (revised edition, ed., G. Ernest Wright and Floyd V. Vilson). Philadelphia: Westminster, 1956. A classic in its field, this volume contains excellent maps, with accompanying articles which introduce each period of biblical history.

Abingdon Maps of Bible Lands (ed., Herbert G. May). New York: Abingdon, 1966. A set of eight maps in a very usable format and based on the most recent scholarship.

The Golden Bible Atlas, Samuel Terrien. New York: Golden Press, 1957. A very popular and fully illustrated atlas presenting the story of Palestine, Egypt, and the Middle East from Bible times to the present.

COMMENTARIES

Bible Guides, 22 vols. (ed., Wm. Barclay and F. F. Bruce). New York: Abingdon, 1966. Offers popular "guides" to the main themes of each book (or group of books) rather than a commentary on the text of each book.

The Daily Study Bible, 17 vols., ed., Wm. Barclay. Philadelphia: Westminster, 1961. A very readable series of New Testament commentaries for laymen by a leading British scholar.

The Interpreter's Bible, 12 vols. (ed., G. A. Buttrick and others). New York: Abingdon, 1952-1957. Volumes I and VII are especially valuable for their introductory articles.

The Layman's Bible Commentary, 25 vols. (ed., Balmer Kelly). Richmond: John Knox, 1959. Concise, reliable, readable, one of the best overall series of commentaries for laymen.

New Testament Commentary (ed., H. C. Alleman). Philadelphia: Fortress, 1936. A good one-volume commentary with brief introductions to each New Testament book—still valuable in spite of its age.

Old Testament Commentary (ed., H. C. Alleman and E. C. Flack). Philadelphia: Fortress, 1948. A companion to the above volume.

The Old Testament Library (ed., G. Ernest Wright and others). Philadelphia: Westminster, 1962 on. English versions of many of the best volumes in "Altes Testament Deutsch" have appeared in this excellent series, along with other original English volumes.

Peake's Commentary on the Bible (ed., Matthew Black and H. H. Rowley). New York: Nelson, 1962. A standard one-volume commentary recently brought up to date under the direction of two leading biblical scholars.

Torch Bible Commentaries (ed., John Marsh and Alan Richardson). London: S.C.M. An outstanding series of commentaries for laymen in 39 volumes.

INTRODUCTIONS

Anderson, Bernhard, *Understanding the Old Testament* (2nd edition). Englewood Cliffs, N.J.: Prentice-Hall, 1966. This book traces the literary and theological development of the Old Testament within the framework of the great drama: The development of Israel as a community. One of the leading introductions to the Old Testament.

Aaseng, Rolf, *The Sacred Sixty-six.* Minneapolis: Augsburg, 1966. Capsule sketches of the main purpose and theme of each book of the Bible.

The Bible Speaks Again: A Guide From Holland (trans., Annebeth Mackie). Minneapolis: Augsburg, 1969. Produced in Holland by a commission of distinguished writers. This exciting new book leads the reader to a deeper understanding of the true nature and purpose of the Bible as it deals with the role of the Bible in our modern world.

Bright, John, *The Kingdom of God.* New York: Abingdon, 1953. Although technically speaking this is not an "Introduction," it doubtlessly has been the one book most widely used for that purpose during the past decade. By tracing the history of this one major biblical concept throughout the Bible, the author presents a most relevant and readable account of the Bible's total scope and message—a masterpiece.

Cullman, Oscar, *The New Testament: An Introduction for the General Reader* (trans.). Philadelphia: Westminster, 1968. A readable introduction into the literary and historical problems of the New Testament writings with some consideration of their theological content.

Davis, W. D., *Invitation to the New Testament.* Garden City, N.Y.: Doubleday, 1966. True to its title, this volume is an exciting invitation to the message of the New Testament and its significance for today.

Ellis, Peter, *The Men and Message of the Old Testament.* Collegeville, Minn.: Liturgical Press, 1962. Written especially for college students, this volume provides insights into the understanding of the Old Testament for all readers.

Introductions to the Books of the Bible (editors). Philadelphia: Westminster, 1958. Brief, reliable introductions to each book of the Bible.

Kee, Young, and Froehlich, *Understanding the New Testament* (2nd edition). Englewood Cliffs, N.J.: Prentice-Hall, 1965. A companion to the volume by Anderson, of comparable thrust and value.

Myers, Jacob, *Invitation to the Old Testament.* Garden City, N.Y.: Doubleday, 1966. A companion to the above volume by Davis, of comparable thrust and value.

Otwell, John, *I Will Be Your God: A Layman's Guide to Old Testament Study.* New York: Abingdon, 1967. In a simple, clear manner the author discusses the most useful techniques of modern biblical scholarship and how they contribute to rendering the Old Testament more relevant and understandable.

Westermann, Claus, *Handbook to the Old Testament* (trans. and ed., Robert H. Boyd). Minneapolis: Augsburg, 1967. Provides an overall view of the vast scope and significance of the biblical message while pointing out relationships within the Old Testament as well as between the Testaments.

——— *Handbook to the New Testament* (trans. and ed., Robert H. Boyd). Minneapolis: Augsburg, 1969. A companion to the above volume.

Westminster Guides to the Bible, 9 vols. (ed., Edwin M. Good). Philadelphia: Westminster. A series of brief introductions to the various "groups of writings" which constitute the Bible (e.g., *Servants of the Word: The Prophets of Israel*) and an appraisal of their significance for the church today

Wright, G. Ernest, and Fuller, Reginald H., *The Book of the Acts of God*. Garden City, N.Y.: Doubleday, 1960. A standard work which uses the finest contemporary biblical scholarship to introduce the entire Bible as the record of God's actions as perceived by believing man. Highly recommended.

HISTORIES

Albright, W. F., *The Biblical Period from Abraham to Ezra*. Pittsburgh: Biblical Colloquium, 1950, PB: New York: Harper, 1963. An outstanding, concise history of Old Testament times.

Bright, John, *A History of Israel*. Philadelphia: Westminster, 1959. A standard work by a scholar of the so-called Albright school with its emphasis on the use of archeology in the study of the Bible.

Filson, Floyd V., *A New Testament History*. Philadelphia: Westminster, 1964. A very comprehensive and readable account of how the church came into being, showing especially the continuity between the ministry of Jesus and the mission endeavors of the apostolic church.

Finegan, Jack, *Light from the Ancient Past* (2nd edition). Princeton University Press, 1954. Emphasizes ancient history and its bearing upon the Bible.

Noth, Martin, *The History of Israel* (2nd edition, trans., Stanley Rudman from the 2nd German edition and revised by P. R. Ackroyd). London: Adam and Charles Black, 1960. A standard work done from the standpoint of the German emphasis on tradition-history.

GENERAL WORKS

Barclay, Wm., *The Life of Christ for Everyman*. New York: Harper (Chapel Books), 1965. A concise, brilliant, and moving portrayal of the life of Christ, taking into full consideration the results of recent biblical scholarship.

———— *The Master's Men*. New York: Abingdon, 1959. An excellent popular treatment of the disciples.

Beare, Francis W., *The Earliest Records of Jesus*. New York: Abingdon, 1962. A concise, nontechnical commentary on the Synoptic Gospels employing the methods of history and source criticism.

Bishop, Jim, *The Day Christ Died*. New York: Harper, 1957. An outstanding novel which truly captures the mood and setting of the crucifixion.

Brown, Robert M., *The Bible Speaks to You*. Philadelphia: Westminster, 1955. An exciting presentation of the Bible's message in terms of the existential questions of our time. Most highly recommended.

Bryant, Robert, *The Bible's Authority Today*. Minneapolis: Augsburg, 1968. In discussing current approaches to the study of Scripture, the author places special emphasis on its meaning and relevance to our contemporary secular culture.

Clements, R. E., *The Conscience of the Nation: A Study in Early Israelite Prophecy*. London: Oxford University Press (*Approaching the Bible* series), 1967. Most helpful to an understanding of the message of the early Israelite prophets within the context of the situation to which they spoke; includes helpful suggestions for classroom use.

Corbett, J. Elliott, *The Prophets on Main Street*. Richmond: John Knox, 1965. The author presents modern paraphrases of some of the messages of the prophets which speak to the burning issues of our day. Biting, satirical, witty, and most relevant.

Dietrich, Suzanne de, *God's Unfolding Purpose*. Philadelphia: Westminster, 1960. A devotional study of the Bible by a noted French scholar. Charts a course through the Bible, showing the unity of God's Word.

———— *The Witnessing Community*. Philadelphia: Westminster, 1958. The author examines what the witnessing community means in the world today by interpreting the Old and New Testament accounts of God's relationship with his people.

Dibelius, Martin and Kummel, Werner G., *Paul* (trans., Frank Clarke). Philadelphia: Westminster, 1953. Reliable and widely used general presentation of Paul, the man, his message, and his thought.

Everyday Life in Bible Times. Washington, D.C.: The National Geographic Society, 1967. A fascinating and beautifully illustrated volume which literally makes biblical persons, places, and times come to life. Includes articles by some leading biblical scholars.

Facet Books: Biblical Series (ed., John Reuman). Philadelphia: Fortress. Brief, brilliant treatments of vital facets of biblical study; some are translations of German works, such as Westermann's *The Genesis Accounts of Creation*.

Filson, Floyd, *Which Books Belong in the Bible*. Philadelphia: Westminster, 1957. A good popular introduction to the study of the canon of the Bible.

Fretheim, Terence, *Creation, Fall, and Flood*. Minneapolis: Augsburg, 1969. An excellent treatment (for laymen) of those most controversial chapters at the beginning of the Bible, placing them in their proper perspective and allowing them to speak their true message.

Fuller, Reginald, *Interpreting the Miracles*. Philadelphia: Westminster, 1961. This volume helps answer many of the basic problems we confront when trying to understand the miracles in today's scientific world.

Gilbertson, Merrill T., *The Way It Was in Bible Times*. Minneapolis: Augsburg 1959. A nontechnical presentation of the customs and folkways of the people of the Bible.

————*Where It Happened in Bible Times.* Minneapolis: Augsburg, 1963. A simplified handbook of biblical geography portraying the geographical setting of biblical events.

Gloege, Gerhard, *The Day of His Coming: Our Times in the New Testament* (trans., Stanley Rudman). Philadelphia: Fortress, 1967. A companion to the Westermann volume listed below, this book presents the full message of the New Testament against the background of the "thousand years" which preceded it and invites the reader to participate in the "day" which climaxes that history.

Harrisville, Roy, *His Hidden Grace; The Origins, Task and Witness of Biblical Criticism.* New York: Abingdon, 1965. A good introduction to biblical criticism and its relation to the task of preaching and teaching in the local church—most reassuring to the layman on his first journey into the world of modern biblical scholarship.

Heaton, E. W., *The Old Testament Prophets* (revised edition). London: Penguin Books, 1961. This popular summary of the teachings of the prophets serves as a good introduction to their religious ideas and their contribution to the faith of the Old Testament.

Holum, John, *Of Test Tubes and Testaments.* Minneapolis: Augsburg, 1965. Originating as a series of articles in a youth magazine, this book by a Christian scientist is designed for those who feel they must choose between the Bible and science.

Hunter, Archibald M., *Interpreting the Parables.* Philadelphia: Westminster, 1960. Presenting the parables in the light of modern scholarship, the author helps the average reader see their meaning for today's world.

———— *A Pattern for Life* (revised edition). Philadelphia: Westminster. The revised edition of a long popular book on the Sermon on the Mount, now including the insights of the most recent scholarship.

Jones, Clifford, *The Bible Today for Those Who Teach It.* Philadelphia: Fortress, 1965. A simple but comprehensive survey of the entire Bible; includes some good charts and maps.

Kallas, James, *The Story of Paul.* Minneapolis: Augsburg, 1966. A very readable summary of the overall pattern and tempo of Paul's life, together with a presentation of the general direction of his thought.

Knight, George A. F., *Law and Grace.* Naperville, Ill.: S.C.M. Book Club, 1962. An excellent popular treatment of the relationship between Law and Gospel in the overall message of the Bible.

Köhler, Ludwig, *Hebrew Man* (trans., Peter Ackroyd). New York: Abingdon, 1954. A fascinating study of the physical and spiritual characteristics of the Hebrew.

Montet, Pierre, *Egypt and the Bible* (trans., Lester Keylock). Philadelphia: Fortress, 1968. Here an authority in the field of Egyptology throws new light on certain sections of the Bible as he shows their relationship to the people, places, and customs of Egypt.

Moule, C. F. D., *The Birth of the New Testament.* New York: Harper, 1962. Dr. Moule shows how the New Testament took shape by focusing attention not so much on the documents themselves as upon the early church whose life they reflect and express.

Muilenberg, James, *The Way of Israel: Biblical Faith and Ethics.* New York: Harper (Harper Torchbooks), 1961. Under this one theme the reader is guided by a master scholar into the heart of the Old Testament. A little gem.

Paterson, John, *The Goodly Fellowship of the Prophets.* New York: Scribner, 1948. Brief but vivid descriptions of the personality, setting, and message of the individual Israelite prophets

———*The Book That Is Alive,* New York: Scribner, 1954. A good, readable introduction to Israel's wisdom literature.

——— *The Praises of Israel.* New York: Scribner, 1950. A study of the Psalms, comparable to the above volume in scope and thrust.

Plastaras, James, C. M., *The God of Exodus;* The Theology of the Exodus Narratives. Milwaukee: Bruce, 1966. In his discussion of the Exodus Narratives, the author not only helps us understand the theology of the Exodus but also makes us aware of the centrality of the Exodus within the Old Testament and its influence upon the New Testament—another example of the fine biblical scholarship currently in vogue within Roman Catholic circles.

Parrott, Andre, *Abraham and His Times* (trans., James Farley). Philadelphia: Fortress, 1968. A period of biblical history which is only vaguely outlined in the Old Testament comes to life as it is illuminated through the findings of archeology.

——— *Land of Christ.* Philadelphia: Fortress, 1968. The entire setting of Christ's life is illuminated as one accompanies the author on a tour of the Holy Land, with photographs, Bible references, and historical and archeological background.

Quanbeck, Philip, *When God Speaks.* Minneapolis: Augsburg, 1968. The author affirms the Bible while considering such issues as history, authorship, canon, variety of writings, biblical languages, etc.

Rendtorff, Rolf, *Men of the Old Testament* (trans., Frank Clark). London: S.C.M., 1968. A convincing new presentation of the great men of the Old Testament by an author belonging to the newest generation of recognized Old Testament scholars—a most interesting and helpful study.

Reuman, John, *The Romance of Bible Scripts and Scholars.* Englewood Cliffs, New Jersey: Prentice-Hall Inc., 1965. An excellent discussion of the task and history of translating the Bible. This book is out of print, but may be available in some libraries.

Richardson, Alan, *The Bible in the Age of Science.* Philadelphia: Westminster, 1961. This book illustrates how the supposed conflict between science and religion has resulted from a failure to grasp the true nature of the biblical message.

—— *A Theological Wordbook of the Bible.* New York: Macmillan, 1955. Offers summaries of the theological meanings of key biblical words.

Smart, James, *The Interpretation of Scripture.* Philadelphia: Westminster, 1961. An excellent introduction to the various approaches to biblical interpretation.

—— *The Old Testament in Dialogue With Modern Man.* Philadelphia: Westminster, 1964. A lively discussion of certain sections of the Old Testament in terms of their relevance for our current situation.

Staack, Hagen, *Prophetic Voices of the Bible.* New York: World, 1968. In this book, based on a very popular television series of the same title, the penetrating voices of the Old Testament prophets speak anew as the author outlines the career, personality, historical background, and basic message of individual prophets.

Stewart, James, *A Man in Christ.* New York: Harper, n.d. A reverent summary of Paul's thought, approached from the standpoint of his religious experience.

—— *The Life and Teaching of Jesus Christ.* New York: Abingdon, n.d. A devotional approach to the Gospel's message concerning the earthly ministry of Jesus Christ, with Bible readings and discussion questions. Suitable for group or individual study.

—— *The Psalms and Their Meaning for Today.* New York: Bobbs-Merrill, 1952. Certain representative psalms are presented in a manner true to the title of this volume

Toombs, Lawrence, *The Threshold of Christianity.* Philadelphia: Westminster (*Westminster Guides to the Bible* series), 1960. A brief but valuable guide to the study of the period between the Testaments.

Westermann, Claus, *A Thousand Years and a Day: Our Times in the Old Testament* (trans., Stanley Rudman). Philadelphia: Muhlenberg (Fortress), 1962. In tracing the meaning and message of all that occurred in the thousand years which reached their climax in "the day" of Christ's coming, the author presents a popular "Old Testament Theology." A companion to the volume by Gloege listed above.

BIBLICAL ARCHEOLOGY

Albright, W. F., *The Archeology of Palestine*. Baltimore: Penguin Books, 1961. An introduction to the aim and workings of biblical archeology by one of the giants in the field.

Bouquet, A. C., *Everyday Life in New Testament Times*. New York: Scribner, 1954. Draws heavily on the findings of archeology to depict everyday life as it was lived in the time of the New Testament.

Heaton, Eric W., *Everyday Life in Old Testament Times*. New York: Scribner, 1956. A companion to the volume by Bouquet listed above.

Kelso, James, *Archeology and Our Old Testament Contemporaries*. Grand Rapids, Mich.: Zondervan, 1966. A readable and warmly human treatment of archeological facts as they relate to some of the major personalities of the Old Testament.

Wright, G. Ernest, *Biblical Archeology* (abridged edition). Philadelphia: Westminster, 1960. The author, a student of the Albright school, presents the major contributions of biblical archeology toward the deepening of our understanding of the biblical narratives. Highly recommended.

THE DEAD SEA SCROLLS

Burrows, Millar, *The Dead Sea Scrolls*. New York: Viking, 1956. One of the earliest comprehensive and reliable discussions of the discovery of the scrolls and their significance for the Christian faith.

Cross, Frank M., *The Ancient Library of Qumran*. New York: Doubleday, 1960. A comprehensive survey of the Dead Sea Scrolls and their significance for the study of the Bible. Most highly recommended.

Gaster, Theodor, *The Dead Sea Scriptures*. Garden City, N.Y.: Doubleday, 1964. A translation of the important documents from Qumran with brief introductions and explanatory notes.

Milik, J. T., *Ten Years of Discovery in the Wilderness of Judaea* (trans., J. Strugnell). London: S.C.M., 1959.

Ringren, Helmer, *The Faith of Qumran*. Philadelphia: Fortress, 1961. In direct and clear fashion the author summarizes and analyzes the thought and faith of the community which gave us the Dead Sea Scrolls, perhaps a bit technical for the uninitiated layman.

Trever, John C., *The Untold Story of Qumran*. Westwood, N.J.: Revell, 1965. An exciting history of the discoveries at Qumran by the first American to examine, study, and photograph the documents after the initial discovery.

Index of Subjects

131

Index of Names

Index of Scripture References